THE

Lenten Kitchen

by

Barbara Benjamin

and

Alexandria Damascus Vali

PAULIST PRESS
New York, NY • Mahwah, NJ

Library of Congress Cataloging-in-Publication Data

Benjamin, Barbara.
    The lenten kitchen / by Barbara Benjamin and Alexandria
Damascus Vali.
      p. cm.
    ISBN 0-8091-3542-6 (paper)
    1. Vegetarian cookery.   2. Lenten menus.   I. Vali, Alexandria
Damascus.   II. Title.
TX837.B46   1994
641.5′66—dc20   94-33152
                                                            CIP

Published by Paulist Press
997 Macarthur Boulevard
Mahwah, New Jersey 07430

Printed and bound in the
United States of America

TABLE OF CONTENTS

ઢ

INTRODUCTION *1*

ઢ

Section I:
GIFTS FROM THE LAND

ઢ

Main Dishes

Baked Goods and Desserts

Section II:
GIFTS FROM THE DAIRY
ৰ

Appetizers and Soups

Section III:
GIFTS FROM THE SEA
❧

INTRODUCTION

‰

We welcome you to *The Lenten Kitchen*. Here the thoroughly modern Christian can find endless joy in preparing for the miracle of Easter. Here the bond between God's abundance and love and our basic need for nourishment and nurturing can be renewed.

In our worldwide search for recipes, we went into the Black Forest for our *Bienenstich* (a delectable bee sting cake we remembered from childhood), to St. Ann's Bay for our Jamaican Pumpkin Soup and to Valencia for our Spanish Onion Pie. No corner of the globe was too far for us. Years were spent collecting the basic information for the recipes. Back in our own kitchens we adapted all we had gathered to our unique purpose: to create a lenten kitchen that reflected our delight in the infinite diversity of God's universe, a kitchen in which people of all cultures could find both familiar and unusual menus.

We hope that, in some small way, *The Lenten Kitchen* is a place where people come closer together, closer to sensing the Holy Spirit that unites us, and closer to the loving God who created us all.

Lent For The Thoroughly Modern Christian

Since the beginning of the Industrial Revolution, some two hundred years ago, we have increasingly lost touch with the source of our basic foods. Today, how many of us ever consider where the flour comes from to make our pancakes or where the sugar comes from to make our syrup? Those who live in a rural area probably have some awareness of how food gets to the table everyday, or we may have read a book or seen a movie on television that gives us a clue. However, the majority of us remain detached from the many interconnections necessary to feed us.

Attempting to affirm those interconnections, one friend of ours found a unique way of saying grace at the evening meal, thanking the Lord for the farmer, the miller, the trucker, and for all the people who helped to bring her dinner to the table.

For our fragmented times, then, the observance of the lenten season may be more about becoming conscious of the foods we *do* eat, where they come from and how we prepare them, than it is about choosing the foods we *do not* eat. We are, after all, always conscious about what we should *not eat:* foods high in cholesterol and saturated oil; foods that may make us fat or increase our blood pressure or make us prone to disease.

Depending less and less upon God as the creator of all our nourishment, both physical and spiritual, we spend more and more time worrying about our physical fitness and the latest "wonder food": broccoli one month, oats another, and always beta carotene in any form; our dietary choices become largely determined by a continually shifting barrage of official test results. Armed with scientific data, we hope to gain control over everything from cellulitis to death. Only when we become overwhelmed by contradictory information do we begin to sense, once again, that our scientific data may not be all we need to make us invulnerable and immortal.

During the lenten season, then, perhaps we thoroughly modern Christians can stop for awhile to do more than choose our foods because of anxiety, fads, and the latest test results. Perhaps we can stop long enough to discern that our good health, both physical and spiritual, has a divine source; stop long enough to contemplate how well the Lord provides for us and meets our needs; stop long enough to rejoice in how the Lord loves us; and stop long enough to spend some time in thanking God.

A Time Of Renewal

As we began our research for *The Lenten Kitchen,* we faced the challenge of developing recipes that would reflect this time of renewal and infinite possibilities. Could we find enough variety and nutrition for the traditional lenten observers and for the Orthodox Christians who celebrate the Great Lent for forty days and are limited on many of those days to only vegetables. At the same time, could we create a kitchen universal enough for everyone to comfortably experiment with meatless cooking, whether in their observance of Lent or in their ordinary preparation of meals? As we faced these challenges, we were overwhelmed with the creative potential of a meatless kitchen, and we, ourselves, gained a renewed appreciation of the Lord's abundance and the significance of Lent. Our faith in a living God who is always providing nourishment and nurturing strengthened. Our gratitude for gifts, both those we had always recognized and those God now revealed to us, intensified.

Cooking always without meat, and sometimes without milk and milk products or fish, we never felt physically deprived or emotionally unsatisfied with the outcome. On the contrary, our awareness of God's abundance was enriched and expanded; and we came closer to understanding the miracle of protection and renewal that Jesus experienced during his time in the desert. That time became for us not a symbol of want but a symbol of plenty, the plenty which meets our needs and is always available to us if we trust in God's love. It was with this new understanding of the lenten season that we met the challenge of creating *The Lenten Kitchen.*

Fasting and Prayer

For many Christians, Lent and fasting have always been synonymous. However, we could find no precise rules in ancient or modern times to establish uniform dietary practices during this season. The one constant we did find, in all times and in all cultures, was the union of fasting and prayer. From Romans 6:14, we gained some insight into the meaning of fasting: *you are not under the law but under grace;* and, again from Romans 14:17: *for the kingdom of God is not food and drink but righteousness and peace and joy in the Holy Spirit.* Fasting, then, during Lent or at any other time, is not an act of religious obedience or endurance, nor an obligation or a tradition. As it is presented in the gospels, fasting is an act of free choice, of willingness, and of humility. It is an expression of human love and of trust in the divine love of God. Contrary to popular thought, we fast not to prove our strength but to become more conscious of our vulnerability and to acknowledge to ourselves our total dependence on God's grace. In the union of fasting and prayer, we can begin to understand the miracle through which less becomes more—the miracle of the loaves and fishes—and we can discern the sustaining presence of the Holy Spirit in our lives.

In Matthew 4:4, Jesus instructs: *One does not live by bread alone, but by every word that proceeds from the mouth of God.* During Lent we have the opportunity to reach more deeply into ourselves in search of this spiritual food which nourishes us.

Food, Fasting, and Redemption

This, then, is the invitation of the lenten season: to prepare ourselves through prayer and fasting to reconcile ourselves with the divine will and regain eternal communion with God. During Lent, we are reminded of our hunger for God, for reconciliation, for communion, for a way back to our lost paradise. The way we are given is the way of Christ in the desert, a way of trust and obedience to God's will. It is a choice which we, like Adam and Jesus, are each free to make.

Adam, surrounded by plenty in a fertile garden, chose to satisfy himself and his vanity. Jesus, surrounded by want and hunger in a desert, chose to trust and obey his Father. Adam, safe and protected from all harm, except the harm he did to himself, separated himself from God. Jesus, physically vulnerable and alone, remained close to his Father and secure in his faith.

In the early church, the observance of Lent was a preparation for baptism. Today, the observance of the lenten season retains much of that sense of preparation for satisfying our hunger to return to communion with God. It is a preparation for rejoicing, each spring, in God's mercy and God's promise of redemption. Above all, it is preparation for celebrating the passion, death, and resurrection of Christ. How better to prepare for this renewal than to become vulnerable, as Christ had been in the desert; to become keenly aware of the difference between physical craving and true spiritual hunger; to turn inward and be nourished by the love of God.

This, then, is the essence of the lenten season: that we eat as we were originally meant to eat, in communion with and in celebration of God's love; and that we come as close as we can to trusting that the nourishment of our spirit will quiet all our mortal cravings.

As we face each new lenten season, we trust that the Spirit which informed our efforts and led us to a deeper understanding of our relationship to food, to God and, especially, to the miracle of the eucharist, will guide you through your own deeply personal search for peace, joy, and communion.

Easter blessings to you and those you love.

Barbara Benjamin
Alexandria Damascus Vali

And out of the ground made the Lord God to grow every tree that is pleasant of the sight, and good for food; the tree of life also in the midst of the garden, and the tree of the knowledge of good and evil.

(Genesis 2:9)

Gifts from the Land

	I	II
Soup:	Tomato Bisque	Jamaican Pumpkin Soup
Main Dish:	Mideastern Mushroom Mold	Shepherd's Pie
Vegetable:	Honey Carrots	Skillet Greens
Salad:	Herbal Tossed Salad	Dilled Cucumbers
Dessert:	Mixed Apple Pie	Snowballs

ॐ

Behold, a young woman shall conceive and bear a son, and shall call his name Immanuel. He shall eat curds and honey when he knows how to refuse the evil and choose the good.

(Isaiah 7:14–15)

Gifts from the Dairy

	I	II
Soup:	Carrot Bisque à l'orange	Herbal Harvest Soup
Main Dish:	Lasagna Milanese	Spanish Onion Pie
Salad:	Zucchini Salad	Sultan's Salad
Dessert:	Bienenstich	Innisfree Plum Strudel

Now as they were eating, Jesus took bread, and blessed and broke it, and gave it to the disciples and said, "Take, eat; this is my body." And he took a cup, and when he had given thanks he gave it to them, saying "Drink of it, all of you; for this is my blood of the covenant, which is poured out for the forgiveness of sins."

(Matthew 26:26–28)

Gifts from the Sea

	I	II
Soup:	Louisiana Gumbo	Down East Clam Chowder
Main Dish:	Seafood Pastry Supreme	Baked Butterfly of Bass
Salad:	Wild Garden Salad	Carrots-Turnips Canadienne
Dessert:	Heavenly Angel Food Cake	Zeppole di San Giuseppe

Gifts from the Land

Section I

ε∂

GIFTS FROM THE LAND

Then Jesus was led up by the Spirit into the wilderness to be tempted by the devil. And He fasted forty days and forty nights, and afterward He was hungry. And the tempter came and said to him, "If you are the Son of God, command these stones to become loaves of bread."

But He answered, "It is written, 'One shall not live by bread alone, but by every word that proceeds from the mouth of God.'"

Matthew 4:1-4

This first section of *The Lenten Kitchen* includes only fruits, vegetables, grains, and their by-products. The menus we have chosen represent lenten meals from all over the world; and many of them have been used by our own families for over four generations. Each recipe was written with an awareness of the nutritional difficulties presented by this portion of the lenten fast, and special effort was taken to develop menus which incorporate basic food values.

The recipes in this section, made from the simplest of ingredients, remind us of the hunger that Jesus suffered in the desert and the first temptation he faced. Here the devil taunts Jesus, hoping that either ego or hunger will sway him: *If you are the Son of God, command these stones to become loaves of bread.*

Jesus is not tempted. Strong in his faith and resolve, he rejects the devil's offer and affirms his commitment to the word of God.

Dolmadakia

Aunt Zoe was the blue ribbon winner for her stuffed grape leaves.
They are the best!

PREPARATION: 1 HR.   COOKING: 1 HR.   YIELD: 20 SERVINGS

1 (8 oz.) jar grape vine leaves
1 C olive oil
1 small onion, diced finely
1 clove garlic, minced
1 bunch scallions, chopped fine
¼ C currants (optional)
1 C lemon juice

¼ C pine nuts (optional)
3 T chopped fresh parsley
  (reserve parsley stems)
2 T fresh dill
3 C water
1 C rice
Salt and pepper to taste

ᴥTO insure tender leaves, rinse each leaf under running warm water. Blanch leaves in a bunch, in boiling water for a second. Drain in a colander. ᴥHEAT oil; saute onion and scallions; add garlic; brown. Add rice and stir frequently until well-coated with oil (about 5 minutes). ᴥADD currants, nuts, parsley, dill, salt and pepper, ½ cup lemon juice and 1 cup of water. Stir; cover and simmer until liquid is absorbed. ᴥPLACE 1 teaspoon rice mixture near stem of each leaf and roll up, lengthwise, folding in edges. ᴥPLACE rolled leaves in a large casserole with remaining oil, lemon juice and 1 cup of water. If more than one layer is needed, place parsley stems between layers. Cover with a plate and simmer for an hour. Add water as needed; continue cooking until tender. ᴥREFRIGERATE before serving. Garnish with lemon slices. ᴥDOLMADAKIA keeps well for a month, properly refrigerated.

Sesame Seed Dip

PREPARATION: 20 MIN.   YIELD: 6-8 SERVINGS

1 (16 oz.) can of chick peas
   (garbanzo beans)
⅓ C ground sesame seeds
   (tahini)
Juice of 2 lemons

3 cloves of garlic, minced
¼ C olive oil
¼ t pepper
¼ t paprika

❖DRAIN chick peas and reserve liquid. Combine chick peas, tahini, lemon juice, garlic, oil and pepper in a blender or electric food processor, and blend until you have a smooth, thick puree. Add a bit of reserved bean liquid, as needed, for desired consistency. ❖PLACE in a shallow bowl and sprinkle with paprika. Serve immediately or cover with plastic wrap and refrigerate until ready for use. Serve as a dip for raw vegetables, or, more traditionally, as a dip for tasted wedges of pita bread.

Basic Vegetable Stock

Growing up in a large family, we learned not to waste any food. To accumulate vegetable juices, save and freeze all liquids from your daily steamed vegetables in a single stock-pot or container. Also, try adding outer lettuce leaves (usually discarded) to basic stock ingredients while cooking.

PREPARATION: 10 MIN.   COOKING: 1 HR.   YIELD: 6-8 CUPS

2 celery ribs, with leaves
3 medium onions, sliced
2 carrots, with leafy tops
   (if available)
8 C tap water or reserved
   vegetable juices

4 sprigs parsley
1 parsnip
(Italian parsley & root may
   be substituted for the
   above two items)

≈IT is preferable, in this case, to leave all the outer scrapings on the vegetables, including onion skins. Therefore, scrub vegetables thoroughly with a vegetable brush. ≈BRING 8 cups water or reserved vegetable juices to a boil and add scrubbed vegetables. ≈WHEN vegetables are very well done, strain off liquid and mash vegetables through a sieve to separate pulp from liquid. Discard pulp.

Creole Soup

PREPARATION: 15 MIN.   COOKING: 1 HR.   YIELD: 6-8 SERVINGS

1 pkg. frozen or 1 lb. fresh tiny whole okra pods	2 stalks celery, chopped
	5 C boiling water
2 C fresh or canned chopped tomatoes	3½ T margarine or oil
	1 t fresh chopped dill
1 diced green pepper	1 t basil
1 medium diced onion	1 t salt
¼ C long grain white rice	¼ t file powder

≈MELT 1½ T margarine in a 6-quart soup pot; add rice, coating with margarine. Add 5 cups boiling water; simmer uncovered for 10 minutes. ≈WHILE rice is simmering, melt remaining margarine in a separate saucepan; add celery, onion and green pepper; saute lightly. Add chopped tomatoes, dill, basil, salt and file powder; continue cooking until all ingredients are blended (about 3 minutes). ≈COMBINE sauteed vegetables with rice; bring to a boil, cover and simmer for 50 minutes. ≈RINSE fresh okra taking care not to prick pod. Add tiny whole okra and herbs; simmer for 10 more minutes.

Crispy Scallion Potato Soup

PREPARATION: 30 MIN.   COOKING: 40 MIN.   YIELD: 6-8 CUPS

9 pared, thinly sliced medium
   potatoes
1 large leek (you may substitute
   equal amounts of onion if
   leek is not available)

2 celery stalk tops
1 T oil
1 clove garlic, diced fine
2 t salt
⅛ t white pepper

1 bunch crisp scallions with tops, finely sliced in rounds

⋟SLICE leek before washing. Immerse sliced leek in a pot of water; swish to remove all traces of sand. Lift leek from water with slotted spoon. This process may have to be repeated two or three times, until rinse water is entirely free of sand. Saute garlic and leek in oil in the bottom of a 4-quart saucepan, until wilted. ⋟ADD sliced potatoes and celery to the saucepan; cover with just enough hot water to cover potatoes. Bring to a boil; lower heat and simmer; cover and cook until water is almost fully absorbed and potatoes are mushy. ⋟SPOON cooked potato mixture into container of an electric blender, or food processor, and blend until smooth. Return soup to saucepan; add seasoning as indicated, or to taste. Keep warm at lowest heat, until ready to serve. Just before serving, garnish with sliced scallions.

Jamaican Pumpkin Soup

Do not discard those Halloween pumpkins!
They can easily be peeled, sectioned, and steamed until soft;
then pureed and reserved for up to two weeks in the refrigerator,
or for up to six months in the freezer.

PREPARATION: 10 MIN.   COOKING: 1 HR.   YIELD: 8 CUPS

3 cans (29 oz.) unseasoned pureed
   pumpkin, or 3 quarts fresh,
   pureed pumpkin
4 C vegetable stock
½ t cumin

1 t ground coriander
⅛ t ginger
1½ t salt
½ t pepper

BRING vegetable stock to a boil. Add cooked pureed or canned pureed pumpkin and spices. BRING to a boil again; simmer on lowest heat for one hour. Add water if soup begins to thicken too much.

Lentil Soup

This was our Good Friday soup for four generations. With a salad,
it became our meal. Because oil was carried in lambskin pouches
in Europe, our customs taught us that the oil was tainted by the
lambskin and was unacceptable for purposes of fasting. In this
tradition, we omitted oil from this recipe for Good Friday
observances and other strict fast days.

PREPARATION: 15 MIN.   COOKING: 1 HR.   YIELD: 6–8 SERVINGS

1 lb. lentils
2 T oil
1 stalk celery, chopped
2 small carrots, sliced
1 small onion, chopped

10 C boiling water
2 cloves of garlic, minced
1 bay leaf
1 t salt
Black pepper to taste

WASH lentils, drain and set aside. In a large saucepan, saute onion in oil until wilted. Add celery, carrots, garlic and lentils and stir until lentils are well-coated. ADD boiling water, bay leaf, salt and pepper and bring to a boil. Cover and simmer for 1 hour or until tender.

Oriental Nut Chowder

PREPARATION: 10 MIN.   COOKING: 2 HRS.   YIELD: 6–8 SERVINGS

¾ C raw, chopped peanuts
4 C cooking liquid from peanuts
6 oz. Tofu, cut into ½" cubes
¼ C chopped celery
¾ C chopped onion
¾ C chopped mushrooms
1 bay leaf
Salt to taste

1 T sesame oil
2 C canned tomatoes
   (two 7 oz. cans)
2 T tahini or chunky
   peanut butter
2 T thick soy sauce
¼ t dried chili pepper

COMBINE peanuts and 5 cups water; bring to a boil. (Raw peanuts will have a musty odor and chalky color while cooking). Lower heat; simmer about 30 min., until peanuts soften. IN soup pot, saute tofu, celery, onions and mushrooms in a tablespoon of sesame oil, until golden. COMBINE cooked peanuts, 4 cups of peanut cooking liquid, and all remaining ingredients with saute mixture. Bring to a boil; lower heat immediately; simmer for 45 minutes.

Scandinavian Pea Soup

*Another soup that can be used as a fully nutritious lenten meal.
The Scandinavian whole peas give variety of texture and color
to the more classic lenten green pea soup.*

PREPARATION: 10 MIN.   COOKING: 90 MIN.   YIELD: 6 SERVINGS

2 C dried, whole yellow peas or
   whole green peas
5 C water
2 T olive oil
3 medium chopped onions

2 whole cloves
¼ t powdered marjoram
½ t powdered thyme
Salt and pepper to taste

PLACE peas in a strainer and wash under running water. In a
6-quart soup pot, combine peas and 5 cups water and bring to
a boil. Continue boiling for a few minutes. Remove from heat,
cover, and let stand for an hour, removing skins as they float to the
surface. RETURN pot to heat, add all remaining ingredients. Bring
to a boil. Cover, lower heat, and simmer until peas begin to fall
apart (about one hour).

Tomato Bisque

*When tomatoes were plentiful in late summer, we rinsed them
and froze them whole, then pureed them as we needed them for
this lenten tomato soup. The fresh taste of these tomatoes
whet the appetite for spring renewal.*

PREPARATION: 10 MIN.   COOKING: 2¼ HRS.   YIELD: 6-8 SERVINGS

1 can (36 oz.) tomatoes or 3 lbs.
   fresh, chopped tomatoes
3 large onions, sliced
3 T oil
2 C vegetable broth or
   2 C vegetable bouillon
   dissolved in 2 C boiling water

1 t marjoram leaves or
   ¼ t powdered marjoram
¼ C freshly chopped parsley
Pinch thyme leaves
Salt & pepper to taste

≈PLACE oil in soup pot and add sliced onions. Cook over medium flame, just until onion slices wilt. ≈ADD tomatoes, spices and herbs; cook over medium heat for 5 min. ≈ADD 2 cups boiling water and 2 cups vegetable bouillon or 2 cups vegetable broth. Bring to a boil; lower heat and simmer for two hours. ≈REMOVE soup from heat and whirl in electric blender or food processor until creamy. Serve with freshly chopped parsley, as a garnish.

≈

VEGETABLES AND SALADS

Calico Rice

PREPARATION: 10 MIN.　COOKING: 30 MIN.　YIELD: 6-8 SERVINGS

2 C rice
2 C boiling vegetable stock or
　2 vegetable bouillon cubes
　dissolved in 2 C boiling water
1 red pepper, diced
1 green pepper, diced
Salt to taste

1 onion, chopped fine
3 T margarine
2 cloves garlic, chopped
　fine
1½ t powdered cumin
½ t powdered coriander

≈PREHEAT oven to 375°. In an oven-proof casserole, melt margarine over low heat on burner of gas range or electric stove. Saute onions and peppers in margarine until tender. ≈ADD rice, garlic and spices and stir until grains of rice are coated with margarine. Add boiling stock and bring to boil over medium-high heat. Stir once, cover tightly, and place casserole in oven for 20 minutes, or until liquid is absorbed and rice is fluffy.

Honey Carrots

PREPARATION: 10 MIN.   COOKING: 10 MIN.   YIELD: 6 SERVINGS

4 C baby carrots or 6 large carrots, cut up
¼ C honey (herb honey, if available)
½ stick melted margarine
1 C water
Optional: add 1 T slivered candied ginger

❧PREHEAT oven to 350°. Clean carrots and steam or microwave in 1 cup of water, until just tender, about 5 minutes. Drain and place carrots in small baking dish. ❧COMBINE honey and margarine; pour over carrots; bake at 350° for 15 minutes.

New England Bean Bake

How good these are without the classic pork base.
Another example of the vast possibilities we discovered
in preparing this book.

PREPARATION: 15 MIN.   COOKING: 6 HRS.   YIELD: 6 SERVINGS

1 lb. dry Navy beans
3 T dark brown sugar
2 t salt
1½ t dry mustard

⅓ C dark molasses
1 whole, large peeled onion
2 whole cloves
2 T cooking oil

❧WASH and pick over beans, discarding discolored ones. Soak overnight in cold water to cover. ❧PREHEAT oven to 325°. Drain beans; cover with fresh water; boil until just tender, approximately 1½ hours. Do not overcook. ❧PLACE oil and clove-studded onion in bottom of 2-quart covered casserole. Add beans with enough cooking liquid to cover. If necessary, boil additional water to add to bean pot to cover beans. ❧ADD remaining ingredients and gently toss together to coat beans. Cover and place in oven for 6 hours. ❧FOR even baking, stir gently every hour to mix beans. Add boiling water, as necessary, if liquid begins to dry out. Remove cover for the final 30 minutes of baking.

Skillet Greens

*If fresh greens are unavailable, frozen greens may be used,
providing they are thoroughly defrosted and drained. Cooking
time should be reduced to two or three minutes, or just until
greens are warm enough to serve. Again, your frozen summer
bounty comes alive to please you in midwinter.*

PREPARATION: 10 MIN.   COOKING: 10 MIN.   YIELD: 4-6 SERVINGS

1 lb. mustard or collard greens, or a mixture of both
1 clove garlic
2 T oil
Salt and pepper to taste

&WASH greens thoroughly in pot of water, until rinse water is
free of sand. Drain greens and chop coarsely. &SAUTE garlic in oil
until just wilted; then add chopped greens, salt and pepper. &TOSS
lightly and cook until just tender.

Dilled Cucumbers

PREPARATION: 5 MIN.   YIELD: 6-8 SERVINGS

2 large unwaxed cucumbers, scrubbed, very thinly sliced
1 t salt
¼ C wine vinegar
2 t sugar
⅛ t pepper
1¼ t fresh chopped dill

&SLICE unpeeled cucumbers. &COMBINE with ingredients; chill
at least 24 hours.

Herbal Tossed Salad

Salad dressing can be made in advance and can be used for several weeks.

PREPARATION: 10 MIN.   YIELD: 6 SERVINGS

6-8 leaves escarole
6-8 leaves romaine
6-8 leaves chicory
12 black olives
1 T chopped fresh herbs
  (parsley, dill, oregano, basil or mint)

½ C olive oil
¼ C vinegar
¼ t dry mustard
¼ t garlic powder
Salt & pepper to taste

WASH and drain greens; chop or tear into bite-sized pieces; place in salad bowl with herbs and olives. Cover and refrigerate. COMBINE oil, vinegar, spices and whisk until thoroughly combined. SERVE salad well chilled. Add dressing immediately before serving.

Picnic Coleslaw

My father, who owned a restaurant, made the best coleslaw in town. This is his secret recipe.

PREPARATION: 15 MIN.   YIELD: 8-10 SERVINGS

3 lbs. white cabbage, shredded
3 carrots, grated
10 sprigs of parsley, chopped fine
1 scallion, with green top, sliced
  in thin rounds
Dash of sugar

2 T mayonnaise (eggless
  during Lent)
3 T oil
2-4 T white vinegar
  (to taste)
Salt & pepper to taste

IN a large bowl, toss together the first four ingredients. IN a small bowl, combine remaining ingredients, and whisk together until a smooth dressing is formed. POUR dressing over coleslaw and toss until the salad is evenly coated with dressing. COVER and refrigerate until ready to serve. Before serving, toss again to incorporate salad with dressing that has settled on the bottom of the bowl.

Mideastern Wheat Salad

Mint is plentiful during the summer months, either from the markets, or from windowsill or backyard gardens. It can be washed, placed in sandwich baggies, and frozen for use the year round.

PREPARATION: 1½ HRS.   YIELD: 6-8 SERVINGS

1 C fine Bulgur
2 C curly parsley, finely chopped
½ C finely chopped scallions
½ C fresh, chopped spearmint
¼ C lemon juice

¼ t cinnamon
¼ t ground cloves
Salt & pepper to taste
¼ C olive oil
3 ripe tomatoes, peeled and
   chopped

❧SOAK bulgur in water to cover for 1 hour. Squeeze out any remaining water by placing bulgur in a cheesecloth. ❧MIX bulgur with parsley and toss with scallions, mint, lemon juice and spices. Refrigerate until well chilled. ❧JUST before serving, toss with olive oil; add tomatoes and serve on a bed of lettuce.

Three-Bean Salad

PREPARATION: 15 MIN.   COOKING: 3 MIN.   YIELD: 8-10 SERVINGS

1 can chick peas (drained)
1 can kidney beans (drained)
1 lb. string beans, cut diagonally
   into one-inch pieces
1 large onion, chopped
½ C olive oil

¾ C wine vinegar
1 T dry basil
1 T dry oregano
1 t garlic powder
Salt & pepper to taste

BRING 1 quart of water to a boil in a deep saucepan. Place string beans in a steam basket or strainer and place in boiling water for three minutes to blanch. Remove string beans from boiling water after three minutes and place in a bowl filled with ice cold water for three minutes. Drain string beans and place in a large mixing bowl. COMBINE chick peas and kidney beans with string beans and toss gently. IN a small mixing bowl, vigorously whisk together oil, vinegar, herbs and spices. Add chopped onion. Pour salad dressing over beans and toss to combine thoroughly. Place salad in refrigerator until ready to serve. The longer it marinates, the better it tastes.

❧

MAIN DISHES

Baked Harvest

PREPARATION: 30 MIN. COOKING: 1½ HRS. YIELD: 6-8 MAIN COURSE

1 eggplant, scrubbed & cut in wedges

4 medium onions, sliced

4 cloves garlic, chopped

2 green peppers, sliced in wedges

4 carrots, sliced ¼" diagonally

1 lb. string beans, left whole

½ lb. yellow summer squash, scrubbed and cut in wedges

½ lb. zucchini, scrubbed & cut in wedges

2 celery ribs, sliced ¼" diagonally

3 potatoes, cut into 1" cubes

5-6 sprigs parsley, washed and chopped fine

1 lb. fresh peas or ½ box frozen peas

¼ C oil

1 lb. can whole tomatoes or 4-6 ripe fresh tomatoes

Salt and pepper to taste

PREHEAT oven to 450°. Place vegetables in a 3-quart covered casserole dish, with potatoes in the center to prevent sticking. Add onions, garlic, parsley, salt and pepper evenly across top of vegetables. Combine tomatoes and olive oil and pour evenly over casserole. ❧COVER and bake in 450° oven until liquid begins to simmer. Lower to 350°; bake until almost done. ❧REMOVE cover and continue baking until vegetables are slightly glazed.

Condiment-Stuffed Peppers

This same recipe may be used to stuff a variety of vegetables, including eggplant, zucchini and tomatoes. These vegetables should be scooped out and their pulp included in the rice mixture. A mixture of three or more stuffed vegetables may be served at one time. It makes a handsome dish.

PREPARATION: 25 MIN.   COOKING: 2½ HRS.   YIELD: 6 SERVINGS

2½ C brown rice
12 large green bell peppers
3 lbs. fresh chopped tomatoes or
  6 C chopped canned tomatoes
1 (8 oz.) can tomato sauce
1 C water
1 C chopped raisins

2 oz. pine nuts (pignoli)
3 medium onions, chopped
2 t fresh or dry mint
  leaves
2 t basil
¼ t cinnamon
3 T vegetable oil
Salt and pepper to taste

❧PREHEAT oven to 350°. Simmer chopped onion in hot oil in a skillet until soft. Add chopped tomatoes; simmer 5 minutes. Slowly stir in rice, so that tomatoes do not stop simmering. Add raisins, pignoli nuts, salt, pepper, mint, basil and cinnamon. Cook 20 minutes. ❧WHILE rice is cooking, wash peppers, cut off tops; remove and discard seeds. ❧FILL peppers with rice mixture and replace lids on peppers. Place peppers in an oven-proof, covered casserole dish. Combine 8 oz. can tomato sauce and 1 cup water and pour over peppers. ❧BAKE, tightly covered, for 1½ hours at 350°. Uncover and bake another ½ hour.

Garden Spaghetti

PREPARATION: 10 MIN.   COOKING: 2 HRS.   YIELD: 6 SERVINGS

1½ lbs. spaghetti
1 lb. shoestring beans, or 1 lb. peas
3 lbs. fresh, over-ripe tomatoes, diced or 1 large can tomatoes
1 clove garlic, minced

2 medium onions, diced
2 t basil
½ t oregano
2-3 T oil
Salt and pepper to taste

ᴥHEAT oil in saucepan; add garlic and onion; saute until golden. Add tomatoes and spices; simmer over low heat until tomatoes are soft and saucy, about 2 hours. ᴥWHILE the sauce simmers, prepare spaghetti and shoestring beans. Wash beans and snap off tips. Steam beans in just enough water to cover, until tender. Drain and reserve. ᴥBRING 4 quarts of water to a boil, with a pinch of salt and a tablespoon of oil. Add spaghetti, bring to a boil again, cooking until softened. Drain and combine with shoestring beans. ᴥSERVE spaghetti and beans on a warm platter; pass sauce in a separate bowl.

Mideastern Mushroom Mold

PREPARATION: 15 MIN.   COOKING: 35 MIN.   YIELD: 4 SERVINGS

1½ C bulgur
1 lb. large quartered mushrooms or whole small mushrooms
3 C hot vegetable stock
6 medium onions, chopped
4 T oil
Salt and pepper to taste

2 T soy sauce
2 T worcestershire sauce
1 t thyme
½ t paprika
½ t marjoram
¼ c vegetable stock or water

ᴥIN a skillet, over high heat, stir 3 chopped onions in 2 tablespoons oil, until well-browned. Scrape the bottom of the skillet, while the onions are being sauteed, and incorporate the brown scrapings into the wilting onions. Add bulgur and brown lightly. ᴥADD the 3 cups of hot vegetable stock; bring to a boil, lower heat and simmer. Cover; allow to steam for 20 minutes; remove from heat for 5 minutes; separate grains by stirring with a fork. ❧IN a separate skillet, saute remaining chopped onion in the remaining 2 tablespoons of oil until light brown; pour ¼ cup vegetable stock or water into pan; add the mushrooms, salt, pepper, soy, worcestershire, and spices; cover, cook over high heat for 10 minutes or until tender. ❧PLACE prepared bulgur in a circle around a large platter. Fill center with mushrooms and serve immediately.

Moroccan Stew

You don't need to invest in a fancy couscous pot to prepare this dish. To improvise a steam-pot for preparation of the couscous, line a colander with double thickness of cheesecloth. Wrap well. Select a very deep pot in which to cook the vegetables and place colander above vegetables, to steam couscous. Place lid tightly on top of pot containing stew and colander.

PREPARATION: 30 MIN.   COOKING: 1¼ HRS.   YIELD: 6–8 SERVINGS

1 C couscous
1 C canned cooked chick peas
  (garbanzo beans)
1 small peeled, cubed sweet potato
½ turnip, peeled and cubed
½ lb. zucchini, cubed
½ lb. frozen artichoke hearts
2 cubed tomatoes
1 onion, cubed
2 carrots, cubed
2 celery ribs, cubed
¼ C dried apricots
Salt and pepper to taste

1 lemon (cut in 8 wedges)
1 cinnamon stick
5 crushed peppercorns
5 cloves
1 t cumin
1 clove garlic (crushed)
1 t cayenne
⅛ t saffron
4 T oil
2 C water
½ C pine nuts (pignoli)
½ C white seedless grapes
  (optional)

COMBINE carrots, onion and celery in a deep stewing pot with 2 tablespoons of oil and saute gently for 5 minutes. Add tomatoes, cinnamon, peppercorns, cloves, cumin, garlic, cayenne, 1½ teaspoons salt, ground pepper and saffron; cover pot and cook over low flame for 10 minutes. Add chick peas, sweet potatoes and turnips to pot. Cover and continue to simmer for 20 minutes. PLACE couscous in a large mixing bowl and soak in 2 cups of cold water for 5 minutes. Stir gently with a fork and place couscous in prepared colander. Place colander over stewing vegetables in pot, cover tightly and steam for 15 minutes. Place steamed couscous in a deep platter; separate grains by rolling couscous, a cupful at a time, between hands with 2 tablespoons of oil. ADD zucchini and artichoke hearts to pot. Return couscous to colander, making sure cheesecloth is still in place; replace colander over vegetables in stewing pot; replace lid and steam another 10 minutes. PLACE couscous in deep serving platter. Spoon stewed vegetables in center of platter; garnish with apricots, grapes and lemon wedges.

Northern Bean Stew

This is a versatile recipe which can also be served as a soup.
To serve this dish as a soup, beans should be cooked until tender,
but liquid should be added during cooking.

PREPARATION: 15 MIN.   COOKING: 1 HR.   YIELD: 6–8 SERVINGS

1 lb. dried Northern beans	2 diced carrots
½ C olive oil	2 T minced parsley
3 T tomato paste (optional)	2 diced stalks of celery
3 medium onions, sliced	Salt and pepper to taste

RINSE beans, cover with water in a saucepan; parboil for 30 minutes. Add olive oil, tomato paste, sliced onion, carrots, parsley, celery, salt and pepper. COOK until tender, or until water evaporates.

Sesame Moussaka

PREPARATION: 30 MIN.   COOKING: 1 HR.   YIELD: 8 SERVINGS

1 large eggplant	2 T sesame seeds
4 grated carrots	1¼ C oil
6 slices of dried bread, cubed	2 cloves garlic, minced
1 (16 oz.) can of garbanzos, with liquid	2½ T salt
¼ to ½ C tahini	½ t pepper
1 finely chopped onion	¼ t cayenne
4 T oil	Two quart oven-proof pan

❧PREHEAT oven to 350°. Grease casserole dish with 1 tablespoon of oil and put aside. Scrub eggplant and slice in thin circles; brush circles with ½ cup oil, less 1 tablespoon; place on foil-lined baking sheet and broil. ❧SAUTE onion in 1 tablespoon oil; add remaining 3 tablespoons of oil and saute bread cubes until golden; add grated carrots, 2 teaspoons salt and ¼ teaspoon pepper to mixture and continue to saute until all ingredients are well blended. ❧BEGINNING with slices of broiled eggplant, alternately layer eggplant and carrot stuffing into prepared casserole dish. ❧USING the container of an electric blender or food processor, blend together tahini, garbanzo with liquid, remaining oil, as needed, garlic, remaining salt and pepper, and ¼ teaspoon cayenne until a thick, smooth dressing is formed. Spread this mixture over casserole, sprinkle with sesame seeds and bake for one hour, or until top is golden brown.

Shepherd's Pie

PREPARATION: 10 MIN.   COOKING: 1 HR.   YIELD: 6–8 SERVINGS

15 medium potatoes, peeled and diced   4 T margarine
2 boxes frozen mixed vegetables   2 t salt
1 C frozen diced yellow turnip   1 t pepper
6 tiny frozen white onions   ½ t garlic powder
2 T oil   2 T paprika
9″ round oven-proof casserole dish or deep pie pan

&PREHEAT oven to 350°. Boil potatoes until tender; mash with margarine, 1 teaspoon salt, ½ teaspoon pepper and ½ teaspoon garlic powder. Reserve. &SAUTE onions in 2 tablespoons oil for 3 minutes. Add mixed vegetables and turnip; saute until defrosted; add remaining salt and pepper. &SPOON vegetables evenly into casserole. Cover vegetables with an even layer of reserved, mashed potatoes. Sprinkle potatoes with paprika. &BAKE in oven for 30 minutes, or until potatoes have a brown, crusty appearance. Serve piping hot.

Skewered Vegetables

2 medium zucchini, cubed
1 pkg. frozen whole pearl onions
   or ¾ lb. fresh pearl onions,
   halved
1 lb. tomatoes, quartered
½ lb. whole, small mushrooms

Salt and pepper to taste
1 green pepper, cubed
1 C oil
Juice of 3 lemons
2 T oregano
2 cloves of garlic, minced

➤PLACE vegetables on wooden skewers, alternating colors to produce a pleasing pattern. Cover—place skewered vegetables in marinade in refrigerator until ready to use, turning once in a while to evenly marinate. ➤PREHEAT oven to 450°. Bake kabobs in hot oven about 7 minutes. Turn when vegetables are slightly browned, but still crisp. Bake for another 7 minutes. ➤SERVE on a pilaf of rice (white and wild rice combined); or other whole grain.

Super Loaf

PREPARATION: 20 MIN.   COOKING: 3¼ HRS.   YIELD 6-8 SERVINGS

½ C uncooked whole grain rye
3 C bread crumbs
1 C uncooked pinto beans
2 chopped onions
1 bunch chopped scallions
1 grated carrot

3 T chopped parsley
½ C flour
2 T soy sauce
1 T oil
4 C water
Salt to taste

≈PREHEAT oven to 350°. Bring 1 cup of water to a boil and add rye; cover and simmer on lowest heat until tender, about 20 minutes. Add liquid if needed. ≈EARLY in the day or the night before, rinse pinto beans thoroughly in a pot of cold water; remove discolored beans with slotted spoon. Soak beans for several hours. (If using canned beans, 2 cups must be substituted for 1 cup uncooked beans, and cooking time will be reduced by 2 hours.) Bring 2 cups of water to a boil; add rinsed beans; bring to a boil again; lower flame and simmer about 1 hour, or until beans are very tender and mushy, about 2½ hours. ≈SAUTE onions, scallions, carrot and parsley in 1 tablespoon of oil, until all ingredients are soft. Add sauteed ingredients to bread crumbs, moistening crumbs first with remaining cup of water and 2 tablespoons of soy sauce. Add cooked rye, pinto beans, flour and salt. ≈SHAPE mixture into a loaf pan; bake for 35-40 minutes, or until lightly browned.

Tostados Frijoles con Salsa de Chili

PREPARATION: 20 MIN.   COOKING: 2½ HRS.   YIELD: 6 SERVINGS

12 whole corn tortillas
1 lb. dried Pinto beans
5 C water
2 medium-sized chopped onions
½ C oil
½ t oregano
1 T chili powder
½ t garlic powder
¼ t cumin (ground)

Salsa de Chili
4 large ripe tomatoes
  (chopped fine)
2 small white onions
  (chopped fine)
1 t ground coriander
2 canned or fresh chilies
  (chopped fine)
1 T oil
6 C shredded crisp lettuce
Salt and pepper to taste

RINSE beans thoroughly in pot of cold water; remove with slotted spoon, discarding discolored beans. Return beans to pot; soak overnight, in enough water to cover, or bring to a boil, cover, and remove from heat for 2 hours. Drain soaked beans and reserve in bowl. IN the bottom of the bean-pot, saute chopped onions in ½ cup of oil, until golden brown, taking care to incorporate brown scrapings in the skillet with the wilting onions. Add the reserved beans, spices and 5 cups of water. Bring to a boil, stir, lower heat and simmer until beans are very tender, about 2½ hours. Remove beans from heat, mash and return to heat until all moisture is absorbed, and beans are of a thick consistency. PREPARE tortillas according to package instructions, and put aside. Combine tomatoes, onions, chilies, spices and oil in a bowl and toss lightly. Put shredded lettuce in a separate serving bowl. FILL each prepared tortilla with ½ cup of bean mixture. Pass bowls of shredded lettuce and chili sauce, for garnish.

Two-Bean Chili

PREPARATION: 5 MIN. COOKING: 45 MIN. YIELD: 6 SERVINGS

4 C cooked soy beans,
  canned or fresh
2 C cooked kidney beans,
  canned or fresh
½ C liquid from kidney
  or soy beans
1 medium onion, chopped

2 T oil
1 T chili powder
½ t cumin
½ t coriander
1 small onion, diced fine
Pepper to taste
2 T tomato paste

➻IN a skillet, brown onion in 2 tablespoons of oil. Combine juice from beans, spices, and tomato paste, and add to skillet. ➻COMBINE soy and kidney beans and stir into mixture in skillet. ➻SIMMER on low flame for 30 minutes, stirring occasionally to prevent sticking. ➻SERVE with rice; garnish with fresh diced onion, if desired.

Vegetable Chow Mein

PREPARATION: 45 MIN.   COOKING: 15 MIN.   YIELD: 6-8 SERVINGS

4 bamboo shoots (optional)
6 water chestnuts
½ lb. bean sprouts
1 green pepper
2 stalks bok choy
1 large carrot
¼ lb. Chinese pea pods or
   tiny frozen peas
3 onions
2 ribs celery
Stems from a bunch of broccoli

2 garlic cloves
1⅛" sliced fresh ginger
2 T peanut oil
1 t sesame oil
¼ C chopped almonds
   (for garnish)
1 C hot vegetable stock or
   water
1 T corn starch or
   arrowroot flour

☙CUT vegetables, Chinese-style, diagonally ¼" × 1½"; onions are to be cut vertically. Keep vegetables separated, until ready to stir fry. ☙HEAT 2 tablespoons of peanut oil in wok, or fry pan; add ginger, stir fry 2 minutes; add garlic cloves, stir fry another minute; remove garlic and ginger; chop and reserve. ☙ADD broccoli, carrots and celery; stir fry for 3 minutes; add onions; stir fry for another minute; add remaining vegetables; stir fry for another 2 minutes. Dissolve starch in hot vegetable stock or water; make a well in vegetables, slowly combining vegetable broth or water with Chow Mein. If desired, add chopped garlic and ginger. ☙STIR fry for another minute and serve immediately over boiled rice. Use almonds as a garnish as desired.

Honey Spice Cake

*This cake lasts at least 4 weeks if stored in airtight cookie tins,
and tastes best when served at least 2 days after baking.*

PREPARATION: 15 MIN.   COOKING: 1¼ HRS.   YIELD: 36 PIECES

4 C unbleached white flour
1 t baking powder
1 t baking soda
1 C oil
2 C water
1 C honey
1 C sugar
1½ t cinnamon
1½ C walnuts, chopped fine
¼ C sliced almonds
8″ × 13″ oven-proof pan, greased
36 paper muffin cups

Syrup
1 C sugar
1 C water
½ lemon
3 T honey

❧PREHEAT oven to 350°. Sift together flour, baking powder and baking soda into a large mixing bowl and reserve. In a saucepan, over low heat, melt margarine and add 1 cup of honey, 1 cup of sugar, cinnamon and walnuts. Bring to a rolling boil, stirring every few minutes. ❧ADD honey mixture to flour mixture and, with a wooden spoon, beat together until thoroughly blended. Spoon batter into greased oven-proof pan and spread evenly, using a moistened metal spatula. Bake in pre-heated oven for 45 minutes. ❧MEANWHILE, combine 1 cup sugar, 1 cup water and ½ lemon in a saucepan. Bring to a boil, lower heat and boil gently for 15 minutes. Remove lemon and stir in 3 tablespoons of honey. Lower heat to warm setting. ❧REMOVE finished cake from oven, leave in pan, and cut the cake lengthwise into 5 strips. Cut each strip diagonally into 7 or 8 diamond shaped pieces. Pour warm syrup evenly over cake and press an almond slice in the center of each diamond. Leave cake in pan until all syrup is fully absorbed (about 3 hours). With a cake spatula or knife, gently lift each diamond out of the pan and place in an individual paper muffin cup. Stack filled muffin cups in airtight cookie tins and reserve until ready to use.

Mixed Apple Pie

PREPARATION: 30 MIN. COOKING: 45–50 MIN. YIELD: 6–8 SERVINGS

2½ C unbleached flour
½ t salt
¾ C margarine
3–4 T refrigerated water
3 Cortland apples
3 MacIntosh apples

2 green apples
¼ C brown sugar
½ t cinnamon
½ t margarine
1 t lemon juice

PREHEAT oven to 450°. Core, peel and slice apples into eighths. Combine with sugar, cinnamon, ½ tablespoon margarine and lemon juice. Reserve while preparing crust. SIFT flour and salt together in mixing bowl. Add half the shortening to the flour with a pastry blender until shortening is broken into pea-sized bits. Add remaining shortening; repeat blending process until mixture is all in pea-sized bits. ADD ice-cold water, 1 tablespoon at a time until all flour is moistened and holds together in a soft ball. Divide ball of dough in half. Flour a board generously and roll out dough to 9 inches. Place in a greased 9-inch pie plate. ARRANGE apples in pie plate. Roll out top crust following same procedure as for bottom crust. Cover apples with top crust. Seal top crust by pressing edge of crust against bottom crust with a wet fork. With a sharp knife, carve a "V" in the center of top crust for the steam to escape. Prick top crust with a fork. Brush with water. Place in 450° oven for 10 minutes. Lower oven to 425° and bake 30–40 minutes.

Snowballs

PREPARATION: 25 MIN.   COOKING: 15 MIN.   YIELD: 3 DOZEN

1 C ground pecans or almonds	½ C superfine sugar
3¾ C flour	1 C oil
½ t cinnamon	1 T cognac or vanilla
1 t unsweetened cocoa	2 C confectioner's sugar

🍃PREHEAT oven to 350°. In a mixing bowl, make a well in sifted flour. Add remaining ingredients. Combine by hand, until well blended. 🍃SHAPE dough into walnut-sized balls. Place on foil-lined cookie sheet. 🍃BAKE at 350° until just brown, about 15 minutes. Sprinkle a wax paper lined surface with ½ cup confectioner's sugar. Place cookies on paper to cool. Sift remaining confectioner's sugar over warm cookies.

Dried Fruit Salad

PREPARATION: 5 MIN.   COOKING: 30 MIN.   YIELD: 8–10 SERVINGS

1½ C dried apricots	4 C water
1 C dried pitted prunes	4 T sugar or honey
½ C dried apple slices	1 stick cinnamon
1 C dried pear halves	¼ lemon

🍃COMBINE sugar, water, lemon and cinnamon in the bottom of a steamer pot. Place dried fruits in strainer section and place over water mixture. 🍃COVER pot and simmer fruits over low heat for 30 minutes, or until fruit is swollen and tender. Do not let fruit become mushy. 🍃REMOVE from heat. Discard cinnamon stick and lemon quarter. 🍃PLACE steamed fruit in a container large enough to hold the fruit and *all* the cooking liquid. Refrigerate for at least 24 hours to allow juices to become partially absorbed and thickened.

Summer Jewels

PREPARATION: 15 MIN.   COOKING: 15-20 MIN.   YIELD 4-6 SERVINGS

3 peaches, pitted and halved
3 pears, cored and quartered
½ lb. large,firm, bing cherries

4 T honey
1 cinnamon stick
1 C water

&PLACE water in a 2-quart saucepan. Add honey and cinnamon stick and bring to a boil. Lower heat. &PLACE fruits in a vegetable steamer basket and insert into pot. Cover and simmer for 15 to 20 minutes, or until fruit is tender. &SPOON fruits into a serving bowl. Pour liquids over fruit. Cover bowl and refrigerate for 2 hours or until ready to serve.

Summer Melon Refresher

PREPARATION: 30 MIN.   YIELD: 8-10 SERVINGS

9 C of mixed summer melon balls
   (choose casabas, cantaloupes,
   honeydews, persians,
   watermelons and papayas,
   to suit your taste)

1½ C firm blueberries
3 T sugar (optional)
⅓ C fresh lime juice
2 T fresh lemon juice
1 t grated lime rind

&WASH and drain blueberries and mix gently with melon balls in a large, decorative bowl. &COMBINE the lemon and lime juices. Add the lime rind and the sugar, if you are using it, and whisk until sugar is fully dissolved. &GENTLY toss the fruit with the citrus syrup until fruits are evenly coated. &COVER bowl with plastic wrap and refrigerate for at least an hour or until ready to serve. Toss gently just before serving to combine fruit with syrup that has settled at the bottom of the bowl.

Gifts
from the
Dairy

Section II

✿

GIFTS FROM THE DAIRY

Then the devil took Him to the holy city, and set Him on the pinnacle of the temple, and said to Him, "If you are the Son of God, throw yourself down; for it is written, 'He will give His angels charge of you,' and 'On their hands they will bear you up lest you strike your foot against a stone.'"

Jesus said to him, "Again, it is written, 'You shall not tempt the Lord your God.'"

Matthew 4:5-6

Eggs, milk and milk products are incorporated into the meals in this second section of *The Lenten Kitchen.* The recipes are richer in proteins than those in the first section, and can be used separately or as a balance for the purely vegetarian meals.

Whatever combination of recipes we use during the lenten season, we should keep in mind that fasting is not an exercise in physical endurance. Along with prayer, it is a path to a deeper spiritual communion with God. If we become overly concerned with the physical rigors of our fast, we may be pushing ourselves past reasonable limits. Inadvertently, we may be doing exactly what the devil wanted Jesus to do in this second temptation. We may be tempting God to give us proof of God's mercy and protection.

Jesus, receiving God's protection with humility, turns away again from his adversary and admonishes against tempting the Lord.

Baked Tomato Surprise

This recipe has proven its versatility as an appetizer or, when doubled, as a perfect brunch or luncheon dish. One fancier of this recipe has suggested that a bed of freshly creamed spinach be substituted for the rice, omitting the peas entirely.

PREPARATION: 10 MIN.   COOKING: 45 MIN.   YIELD: 4 SERVINGS

4 medium-large tomatoes	1 T dried parsley
4 medium-large eggs	½ t dried basil
1 C long grain rice	1 T butter
1 (10 oz.) package frozen peas	1 t salt
2 t grated Romano cheese	¼ t pepper
2 t grated Parmesan cheese	

ﻩPREHEAT oven to 375°. Wash and core tomatoes. Cut a very thin slice off the top of each tomato and reserve. Scoop out tomato pulp with a large spoon, taking care not to puncture bottom or side walls. Finely chop or puree in processor the reserved top slices and pulp. Place chopped or pureed tomato pulp in a small saucepan, add basil and simmer on low heat until thickened (about 15 minutes). ﻩPLACE scooped out tomato shells in a greased baking dish and season insides with ½ teaspoon salt and ¼ teaspoon pepper. Gently crack eggs, taking care not to break the yolks, and drop an egg into each scooped out tomato shell. Top eggs with thickened tomato puree. Combine Romano and Parmesan cheese and place 1 teaspoon in each tomato cup. Bake in oven 30 minutes for soft eggs, 40 minutes for hard eggs. ﻩMEANWHILE, bring 2 cups water to boil with ½ teaspoon salt. Add rice, butter and parsley. Bring to a boil again, stir once, lower heat, cover, and steam until rice is tender (about 20 minutes). Place frozen peas in a saucepan, add *no water,* cover and steam on low heat for 15 minutes, or until peas are heated through. ﻩARRANGE a bed of rice on individual plates and surround with peas. Make a well in the center of each rice bed. When eggs are baked to desired consistency, remove from oven and gently place an egg-filled tomato cup on each rice bed. Serve immediately.

Crisp Cheese Squares

PREPARATION: 1 HR.   COOKING: 1 HR.   YIELD: 4 DOZEN PIECES

1 lb. small curd cottage cheese, regular or light
1 lb. feta cheese, diced fine
1 (8 oz.) package cream cheese, regular or light
1 egg, beaten
Salt & pepper to taste
1 lb. phyllo pastry sheets
½ lb. butter, melted

❧IN a large bowl, mix together cream cheese, feta and cottage cheese. Add beaten egg, salt and pepper and combine thoroughly with cheeses. ❧PREHEAT oven to 300°. Butter a 8″ × 13″ oven-proof baking pan and set aside. ❧BRUSH one sheet of phyllo with melted butter. Place in pan. Continue procedure using ½ of the phyllo. Place filling evenly across phyllo in pan and continue buttering each sheet and placing in pan until all the sheets are used. With serrated knife, cut through 24 squares. ❧BAKE in preheated oven for an hour or until crisp and golden.

Eggplant Caviar

PREPARATION:15 MIN.   COOKING:15 MIN.   YIELD:10–12 APPETIZERS

1 eggplant
2 hard boiled eggs, diced fine (optional)
4 T mayonnaise
¼ C olive oil
3 T fresh lemon juice
1 Kosher dill pickle, chopped fine
3 cloves garlic, diced fine
1 small onion, diced fine
5 sprigs parsley, chopped
Salt and pepper to taste

ɚSCRUB eggplant and place on baking sheet in 375° oven for about 20 minutes, or until skin begins to wrinkle and a fork can easily pierce to the center of the eggplant. Remove from oven, peel and discard skin and mash eggplant. ɚADD all remaining ingredients and toss gently until thoroughly combined. Place in a serving crock, cover with plastic wrap and refrigerate until ready to serve. The longer this dish marinates the better. ɚSERVE eggplant caviar with crisp, thin sesame crackers.

Spanikopeta

PREPARATION: 1 HR.   COOKING: 1 HR.   YIELD: 2 DOZ. PORTIONS

2 pkgs. (10 oz.) frozen, chopped
    spinach, defrosted and drained
1 lb. phyllo pastry sheets
2 sticks butter, melted
1 medium onion, chopped
1 bunch scallions, with green
    tops, chopped
Salt & pepper to taste

1 bunch parsley, chopped
    fine
2 C feta cheese, diced fine
6 eggs, beaten
¼ C olive oil
1 T dill, chopped (optional)
8″ × 13″ oven-proof pan

ɚPREHEAT oven to 375°. Heat oil in a small skillet and saute onions and scallions until translucent and limp. Do not brown. In a large bowl combine spinach, sauteed onions and scallions, parsley, dill, feta cheese and beaten eggs. Add salt and pepper to taste. ɚBRUSH oven-proof pan with butter. Place a pastry sheet over bottom of pan and brush with melted butter. Repeat process, using 9 pastry sheets. Place spinach mixture evenly over pastry sheets. ɚPLACE a pastry sheet over the spinach mixture and brush with melted butter. Repeat process, using up remaining pastry sheets. With a sharp knife, score the pastry sheets into 24 two-inch squares. ɚPLACE in preheated oven and bake for 50 minutes or until crust is flaky and golden.

Carrot Bisque à l'orange

PREPARATION: 15 MIN.   COOKING: 1 HR.   YIELD: 4 SERVINGS

1 quart vegetable stock
8 medium carrots, sliced
2 t orange rind
6 thin strips of orange peel
   (for garnish)
½ C freshly squeezed orange juice
2 medium onions, chopped
1 small clove garlic, minced fine

4 springs of parsley,
   chopped
2 T light butter
4 t rice, uncooked
⅛ t sugar
½ t salt
1 egg yolk (optional)
4 T light cream (optional)

&IN a soup pot, over low heat, combine carrots, onions, garlic and rice with margarine and stir until vegetables and rice are well coated with margarine and onions begin to wilt (about 4 minutes). Add vegetable stock and bring to a boil. Lower heat, and stir in parsley, orange rind, sugar and salt. Cover and simmer for half an hour. &IN an electric food processor, or blender, puree soup, two cups at a time. Pour pureed soup back into soup pot. Add orange juice and reheat soup. Do not boil. &(OPTIONAL)—Beat egg yolk and light cream together in a small bowl. Whisking vigorously, mix ¼ cup of hot soup into egg mixture. Very slowly pour egg mixture into soup pot, whisking soup vigorously to prevent egg from curdling. &SERVE hot. Garnish each bowl with a thin strip of orange peel.

Creamy Almond Bisque

PREPARATION: 15 MIN.   COOKING: 1 HR.   YIELD: 6-8 SERVINGS

1 large potato, diced
1 large onion, diced
6 stalks celery, diced
1½ C blanched slivered almonds
5 C vegetable stock or water
2 T butter

1 T flour
½ C milk
1 bay leaf
4 sprigs parsley
Salt and pepper to taste

≈IN a 2-quart saucepan, combine vegetable stock, potato, onion, celery, bay leaf and parsley and cook until potato is nearly falling apart. ≈WHILE potato is cooking, place 1 cup of slivered almonds in processor or blender and grind until nuts are powdery fine. When potato is ready, add ground nuts to saucepan and gently simmer for half an hour. Remove bay leaf and cool slightly. Place remaining ½ cup of almonds on a cookie sheet and toast in oven at 350° until lightly tanned. Reserve for garnish. ≈PLACE soup in processor or blender and puree until creamy smooth. ≈MELT butter over low heat. Remove from heat and vigorously whisk in flour until smooth. Whisk flour mixture into strained soup. Return soup to heat and bring to a boil, while continuing to whisk. Season with salt and pepper to taste. Just before serving, swirl 1 tablespoon of milk into each bowl. Serve hot or cold with toasted almonds for garnish.

Herbal Harvest Soup

PREPARATION: 20 MIN.   COOKING: 40 MIN.   YIELD: 4-6 SERVINGS

4 carrots, diced	2 t flour
3 leeks, sliced (whites only)	1 t dried parsley or
1 C cauliflower, in florets	1 T fresh
½ C peas	1 t dried mint or 1 T fresh
½ C string beans, cut in	1 t dried summer savory or
diagonals	1 T fresh
3 C water or vegetable stock	1 t dried thyme or
1¼ C skimmed milk	1 T fresh
2 T butter	1 t dried basil or
1 egg	1 T fresh
2 t salt	¼ t white pepper

≈IN a large saucepan, melt butter over low heat and add leeks and carrots, stirring to coat them evenly with melted butter. Continue stirring for 3 minutes. Add the flour and blend by stirring for another few minutes. Add the water or vegetable stock. Stir for a few minutes to blend ingredients. ❧WHILE continuing to stir, bring soup to a boil and add 1 cup of milk, remaining vegetables, herbs and spices. Stir once more, cover and simmer gently until vegetables are tender, about 15–20 minutes. Remove from heat. ❧IN a small bowl, whisk together egg and remaining ¼ cup of skimmed milk until well blended. While whisking vigorously, add 2 tablespoons of hot stock to the egg mixture and repeat process until you have incorporated a full cup of stock into the egg mixture, 2 tablespoons at a time. Very gradually blend egg mixture into soup pot, whisking continuously as you do this. ❧RETURN soup pot to very low heat. Stir continually and simmer gently for 5 minutes. Serve piping hot.

❧

VEGETABLES AND SALADS

Innisfree Potato Pie

PREPARATION: 20 MIN.   COOKING: 1½ HRS.   YIELD: 6–8 SERVINGS

10 medium size potatoes, boiled	2 T oil
1 lb. mushrooms, sliced	2 t salt
2 medium onions, chopped	½ t pepper
1 pint sour cream	Paprika
½ C regular or non-fat skim milk	10″ deep dish pie plate
4 T butter or margarine	or 10″ ceramic quiche
	baking pan

❧PREHEAT oven to 375°. Mash potatoes and whip until smooth with butter, milk, 1 teaspoon salt and ¼ teaspoon pepper. Grease and line pie plate with half the potato mixture. ❧HEAT oil in a medium sized saucepan and saute onions until lightly browned. Add sliced mushrooms, 1 teaspoon salt and ¼ teaspoon pepper and saute for 15 minutes or until mushrooms are tender. ❧WITH a slotted spoon, lift sauteed mushroom mixture out of saucepan and layer over potatoes in pie plate. Follow this with a layer of sour cream, using the full pint. Top the sour cream with the remaining potatoes, sprinkle with paprika and bake 30 to 40 minutes until top crust of potatoes is evenly browned. Serve immediately.

Marinated Asparagus

PREPARATION: 10 MIN.   COOKING: 15 MIN.   YIELD: 4-6 SERVINGS

2 lbs. fresh asparagus spears
¼ C olive oil
3 T fresh lemon juice
½ t salt
Dash of pepper

≈SNAP off the tough ends of the asparagus stems and discard. Place in asparagus steamer with 2 cups of water. Secure lid to steamer, bring water to a boil, lower heat and steam for 10 minutes, or until asparagus are crisp and tender. Drain, cool and place in a shallow serving bowl. ≈WHILE asparagus are steaming, briskly whisk together the oil, lemon juice, salt and pepper until well combined and thickened. ≈SPOON the marinade over the asparagus. Allow to stand for 15 minutes before serving.

Sultan's Salad

PREPARATION: 15 MIN.   YIELD: 6-8 SERVINGS

1 head Boston lettuce,
    torn in bits
2 endive, sliced thin
3 scallions with green tops, sliced
½ C black pitted olives, sliced
3 T honey

¼ C olive oil
¼ C wine vinegar
½ t parsley
½ t dry mustard
¼ t salt
Dash of fresh ground pepper

COMBINE honey, oil, vinegar, parsley and spices in a mixing bowl or blender container and whisk vigorously until well-combined. GENTLY toss prepared salad greens and olives together in a salad bowl. Pour dressing over salad and toss again to fully coat greens with dressing. SERVE immediately on individual salad plates.

Zucchini Salad

PREPARATION: 15 MIN.   YIELD: 6-8 SERVINGS

2 unpeeled zucchini, sliced
  in thin rounds
1 unpeeled summer squash,
  sliced in thin rounds
1 unpeeled cucumber, sliced
  in thin rounds
8-10 small cherry tomatoes
1 small red Spanish onion, diced
½ C olive oil

¼ C wine vinegar
1 t dry basil or
  1 T fresh chopped basil
1 t dry oregano or
  1 T fresh chopped oregano
½ t garlic powder
Dash of freshly ground
  pepper

GENTLY toss together zucchini, summer squash and cucumber slices in a large salad bowl. IN a mixing bowl, vigorously whisk olive oil, vinegar, herbs and spices until slightly emulsified. Stir in chopped red onion. POUR dressing over salad and toss to evenly coat salad ingredients. Place cherry tomatoes around salad bowl for garnish.

Baked Eggplant Crown

PREPARATION: 40 MIN.   COOKING: 1½ HRS.   YIELD: 8 SERVINGS

3 C large elbow macaroni
2 qts. whole canned tomatoes,
    drained and chopped or
    12–15 large, ripe, fresh
    tomatoes, chopped
1 very large eggplant, at least
    10" long
1 lb. mushrooms, sliced
¼ lb. grated Romano cheese
¼ lb. grated Parmesan cheese
2 eggs, beaten

2 C Italian flavored bread
    crumbs
½ C plus 2 T olive oil
1 T cooking oil
6 oz. margarine
2 cloves garlic, minced
1 large onion, diced
2 t oregano
1 T chopped parsley
1 t basil
Salt and pepper to taste
10" × 3" tube pan

🍃IN a large pot, bring 6 quarts of water and 1 teaspoon of salt to a rapid boil. Add macaroni and 1 tablespoon of cooking oil to boiling water. Bring to a boil again, lower heat and boil slowly until macaroni is tender. Blanch, drain and reserve. 🍃IN a medium saucepan, heat 2 tablespoons olive oil, add diced onion and saute until transparent. Add minced garlic and saute 2 minutes. Add sliced mushrooms, and saute until wilted. Combine tomatoes, herbs and spices and add to saucepan. Stir ingredients, bring to a boil, reduce heat and simmer, uncovered, for about 30 minutes. Stir occasionally to prevent sticking. Combine 3½ cups of the sauce with macaroni, stir in Parmesan and Romano cheeses. Keep remaining 2½ cups of sauce on low heat. 🍃PREHEAT broiler to 325°. Peel eggplant and slice as thin as possible lengthwise. Dip slices into beaten eggs and then into seasoned bread crumbs. Grease two baking sheets and place eggplant slices on them. Brush a teaspoon of olive oil on each slice of eggplant and place in oven. Broil for 15 minutes, or until eggplant slices are slightly browned on both sides. ❧PREHEAT oven to 375°. Thickly coat bottom, sides and tube of a 10″ × 3″ tube pan with margarine. Starting with the bottom, line the tube pan with the eggplant slices. Overlap slices to form a tight lining, running eggplant up the tube and sides of the pan so that each strip of eggplant has a 2½ inch flap hanging over. Fill the lined pan with the reserved macaroni mixture. Use a spoon to firmly pack the macaroni in the mold. Cover the macaroni with the 2½ inch flap. Brush with oil and bake in preheated 375° oven for half an hour. ❧REMOVE mold from oven. Gently loosen eggplant from sides of the pan with a metal spatula. Place a 12-inch heated serving platter over mold and let stand for 15 minutes. Meanwhile, reheat reserved sauce, and place in a gravy server. Invert mold onto platter. Serve immediately with reserved sauce for individual taste.

Gala Cheese Casserole

PREPARATION: 25 MIN.   COOKING: 1 HR.   YIELD: 6–8 SERVINGS

½ lb. spinach macaroni
½ lb. farmer cheese
½ lb. feta cheese, diced fine
3 eggs
1 C milk
3 T Parmesan cheese, grated

3 T Romano cheese, grated
10 T butter, melted
8 sheets of phyllo pastry
   leaves
Salt & pepper to taste
1 two-quart, oven-proof pan

❧IN a large pot, bring macaroni to a rapid boil in 5 quarts of water. Lower heat and boil gently for 7 minutes, or until macaroni is just tender enough to pierce with a fork. Drain macaroni and place in a large bowl. ❧BEAT one egg and slowly add 1 cup milk and 2 tablespoons melted butter, beating until well combined. Add in salt and pepper. Combine this mixture with the macaroni and reserve. ❧THOROUGHLY mix together the farmer cheese and feta. Beat the remaining two eggs and combine with the cheese mixture. ❧PREHEAT oven to 350°. Brush pan with butter and line bottom of the pan with one sheet of phyllo pastry cut in half. Brush the

½ sheet of pastry in the bottom of the pan with butter and repeat process with the other half of the pastry sheet. Take a second sheet of pastry and center it in the pan so that it overlaps on both sides of the pan. Brush the bottom and sides of the phyllo in the pan with butter. *Do not butter the overlap.* Repeat process using two more sheets of pastry. ❧EVENLY spread half of the reserved macaroni, egg and milk mixture in the pan. Combine the grated Parmesan and Romano cheese and sprinkle half of this mixture over the macaroni. Evenly spread the farmer cheese and feta mixture over the macaroni, using a metal spatula or knife to make sure all the macaroni is covered. ❧ADD the remaining macaroni in an even layer over the cheese mixture. Sprinkle remaining Parmesan and Romano cheese over the macaroni. Fold overlapping pastry sheets, one at a time, over macaroni, brushing each sheet with butter before folding over the next sheet. ❧CUT remaining four pastry sheets in half, place a half sheet over the casserole, and brush with butter. Repeat process until all pastry sheets are used up. With a sharp knife score through the layers of pastry sheets to make six or eight equal portions. ❧PLACE in preheated 350° oven for an hour, or until pastry is crisp and browned. Remove from oven and serve immediately.

Lasagna Milanese

PREPARATION: 30 MIN.   COOKING: 1 HR.   YIELD: 6-8 SERVINGS

¾ lb. flat lasagna noodles
1½ lbs. ricotta cheese (regular or light)
2 eggs, beaten slightly
¼ C grated Parmesan cheese (optional)
8 oz. mozzarella cheese, grated (regular or light)
1 pkg. frozen chopped spinach, defrosted and drained
1 (8 oz.) can tomato sauce
3 T cooking oil
1 t oregano
4 t salt
Pinch nutmeg
1 clove garlic, minced fine
1 medium size onion, chopped
9″ × 13″ baking pan

꒜PREHEAT oven to 350°. In a large pot, bring 2 teaspoons of salt and 6 quarts of water to a rapid boil. Add 1 tablespoon cooking oil to water, to prevent noodles from sticking, and place lasagna noodles in the boiling water. Bring to a rapid boil once again, lower flame and continue slow boiling until noodles are tender (about 15 minutes). Drain, blanch and reserve. ꒜WHILE noodles are cooking, heat the remaining 2 tablespoons of oil in a saucepan, add the chopped onion and saute until translucent. Add the minced garlic and cook for 2 minutes. Next, combine the chopped, defrosted and drained spinach with the onions in the saucepan, season with the remaining two teaspoons of salt and a pinch of nutmeg, and saute until thoroughly heated. ꒜IN a bowl, thoroughly combine the ricotta cheese with two eggs and ¼ cup of grated Parmesan cheese. ꒜GREASE the baking pan and line the bottom with a layer of lasagna noodles. Follow with a layer of the spinach mixture, a layer of the cheese mixture, and then a layer of grated mozzarella cheese. Repeat again, placing a layer of lasagna noodles over the mozzarella, followed by a layer of spinach, ricotta and mozzarella. Finish with a third layer of lasagna noodles. Combine tomato sauce with one teaspoon oregano and pour over casserole. Bake at 350° for 30 minutes, or until bubbly.

Mushroom-Rice Bombe

PREPARATION: 15 MIN.   COOKING: 1 HR.   YIELD: 6-8 SERVINGS

3 C long grain rice
6 C vegetable stock or water,
   heated
1½ lbs. small mushrooms, sliced
1 onion, chopped
¾ C grated Romano cheese
¾ C grated Parmesan cheese

2 T parsley, finely chopped
1½ sticks butter or margarine
2 t salt
2 extra-large roasted red
   peppers
1 (10 oz.) package frozen peas
1 greased, two quart
   oven proof bowl

PREHEAT oven to 350°. In a large saucepan, heat oil and saute the onion until lightly brown. Add sliced mushrooms and salt and continue sauteing until tender. Slowly add rice to saucepan, stirring to combine with mushrooms and coat grains with oil. Add heated water or stock. Stir and bring to a boil. Stir once again, lower heat, cover and steam rice until tender but still very firm. Remove from heat. COMBINE Romano and Parmesan cheeses. Reserve ¾ cup. Mix rice with remaining ¾ cup grated cheese, 1½ sticks of butter, less one tablespoon, and chopped parsley. Adjust seasoning to taste. Place rice mixture in greased, oven-proof bowl and pack down tightly. Place bowl in a large pan in oven and add 2 inches of water to pan. Bake for ½ hour. WHILE bombe is baking, place frozen peas in a small saucepan or microwave and heat. *Do not add water* (peas will steam in the liquid that results from defrosting). Stir once or twice to insure even heating. When heated through, add 1 tablespoon of butter or margarine. REMOVE rice bombe from oven and cool for 3 minutes. Invert onto a large heated round serving platter. Surround bombe with peas and garnish with strips of freshly roasted red peppers, placed lengthwise from crown to base of bombe. Pass remaining grated cheese.

Spanish Onion Pie

PREPARATION: 20 MIN.   COOKING: 1 HR.   YIELD: 6-8 SERVINGS

4 oz. cream cheese, at room
   temperature
1 stick margarine, at room
   temperature
1 C all-purpose flour
3 lbs. Spanish onions, sliced
   thin (red variety)
4 eggs, beaten
⅓ C milk

1⅓ C yogurt
2 T butter or margarine
1 t chopped parsley
½ t chili powder
½ t salt
¼ t black pepper
½ roasted red pepper, cut
   in strips for garnish

BLEND together cream cheese, one stick of butter or margarine and flour until fully combined. With a floured wooden spoon, or with your fingers, press dough into a lightly greased 10″ ceramic quiche pan. Prick and refrigerate. MELT 2 tablespoons margarine in a heated skillet and add onions. Saute until onions are very limp and translucent, but not browned. Remove from heat and cool to room temperature. PREHEAT oven to 375°. In a saucepan, over low heat, combine eggs, yogurt and milk. Add parsley and seasoning and adjust to taste. Combine cooled onions with custard mixture and turn into the quiche shell. BAKE pie in preheated oven for 45 minutes or until golden. Garnish with strips of roasted peppers. Serve immediately.

BAKED GOODS AND DESSERTS

Alsatian Plum Cake

PREPARATION: 30 MIN.   COOKING: 35–40 MIN.   YIELD: 12 SERVINGS

2½ lbs. Italian plums, pitted
   and cut in half
   (or any seasonal fruit)
2 C unbleached white flour
1 C walnut or pecan meal
3 eggs
¾ C skimmed milk

2 sticks (½ lb.) butter,
   at room temperature
3 t baking powder
¼ t salt
¼ t almond extract
1½ T cinnamon
1⅔ C sugar
9″ × 13″ baking pan, greased

PREHEAT oven to 375°. Sift together flour, nut meal, ⅓ cup of sugar, baking powder and salt. IN a separate bowl, whisk together eggs and milk. Make a well in the flour and add 1 stick of the softened butter, the egg mixture and almond extract. Knead together until all ingredients are well combined and dough forms a ball. Press dough into the greased baking pan with a well-floured wooden spoon or fingers, lining the bottom and sides of the pan evenly. **ARRANGE** plum halves in rows, skin side down, pressing them into the dough and overlapping them so that they almost stand on end. **BLEND** together the remaining stick of softened butter, the remaining 1⅓ cups of sugar and the cinnamon. Crumple mixture over plums and bake in preheated 375° oven for 35 to 40 minutes, or until cake is brown and top is bubbly.

Bienenstich (Bee Sting Cake)

This recipe was researched like a PhD. thesis.
With only childhood memories of this heavenly German pastry
to guide us, we tried to re-create the original, but to no avail.
Our research would have to go further. So we enlisted the
assistance of several of our neighbors who still had relatives living
in Germany. After many false starts, with many recipes received
from the homeland, we had success. The final results, which we
guarantee are identical to the magnificence of the original,
came from a dear friend who, while visiting her aunt in the
Black Forest, was able to coax the old woman into revealing
the centuries-old secret of classic Bienenstich.

PREPARATION: 15 MIN.   COOKING: 1 HR.   YIELD: 10 PORTIONS

⅔ C sweet butter, at room temp.	*Glaze:*
⅔ C sugar	¾ C sliced almonds
2 eggs	½ C sugar
2¾ C unbleached white flour	¼ C honey
⅔ C milk	¼ C milk
4 t baking powder	¼ C sweet butter
¼ t salt	
10″ round springform cake pan, buttered	

IN a small saucepan, over low heat, melt ¼ cup butter and add all remaining ingredients for glaze. Stir every few minutes until ingredients make a rolling boil. Remove from heat and set aside to cool. **PREHEAT** oven to 375°. While glaze is cooling, beat butter with an electric mixer or food processor until creamy. Add sugar and eggs and continue beating until fluffy. Sift together flour, baking power and salt and beat into butter and egg mixture. Add milk, beating until a smooth cake batter is formed. ⵦWITH a rubber spatula, turn cake batter evenly into buttered springform pan. Smooth cooled glaze over cake batter and place in preheated oven for about 35 minutes, or until glaze is crackly and golden brown. ⵦREMOVE from oven, cool for 5 minutes and remove sides of pan. If you plan to fill the cake with cream, wait until the cake is thoroughly cooled before attempting to cut through the layer. ⵦ(OPTIONAL)—This heirloom recipe from the Schwarzwald can be converted from a centuries-old coffee klatch delicacy to a special occasions dessert by splitting the cake across the middle and filling it with 1½ cups of vanilla patisserie cream or 1½ cups of whipped heavy cream flavored with a quarter teaspoon of vanilla.

Hot Cross Buns

PREPARATION: 3 HRS.   COOKING: 25 MIN.   YIELD: 20 BUNS

¾ C scalded milk
⅓ C soft butter or margarine
⅓ C sugar, sifted
3½ C flour, sifted
2 eggs, well beaten
1 pkg. active dry yeast,
    dissolved in ¼ C warm water

¾ t vanilla
½ t cinnamon
½ t allspice
1 C, mixed, currants & diced
    dry fruit, soaked & drained
1 T hot milk
1 C confectioner's sugar

ⵦPOUR scalded milk over butter, sugar and salt. Stir until melted and slowly add eggs and ½ teaspoon of the vanilla. Stir until mixture is lukewarm and add dissolved yeast. Stir until blended. ⵦCOMBINE cinnamon and allspice with flour and slowly blend half of flour mixture with liquid. Add currants and fruit and mix well. Add remaining flour mixture, beating until dough is smooth. ⵦTURN dough onto floured cloth, and very gently knead for 3 minutes. Place dough in well-greased large bowl, cover with a cloth and keep in a warm spot until dough doubles in size. ❧KNEAD risen dough again on floured cloth for 1 minute, replace dough in bowl, cover, and leave to double in size again. ❧CUT risen dough in 20 equal pieces. Shape into round buns with hands, and place on 10″ × 14″ greased baking sheet. With sharp knife, cut a small cross in top of each bun. Let rise another 45 minutes, until doubled in size, then bake in a preheated 350° oven. ❧COMBINE, for icing, 1 tablespoon hot milk with remaining ¼ teaspoon vanilla and add about 1 cup sifted confectioner's sugar to desired consistency. ❧PIPE icing in cross design on cooled buns through a No. 6 tube.

Innisfree Plum Strudel

PREPARATION: 50 MIN.   COOKING: 50 MIN.   YIELD: 2 STRUDELS

1 lb. phyllo sheets
1½ lbs. sweet butter, melted
2 C blanched almonds,
    ground to a powder
2 lbs. fresh or frozen Italian
    plums or seasonal fruit
¾ C golden raisins

1 C dry white wine
¾ C slivered almonds,
    chopped coarsely
¾ C sugar
2 t cinnamon
¼ C confectioner's sugar

❧SOAK raisins in white wine until plump. Meanwhile, remove pits from plums. Do not peel. Dice each plum into 12 pieces. Drain off any juices which accumulate while dicing. Drain raisins and combine thoroughly in a medium size bowl with diced plums, chopped slivered almonds, sugar and cinnamon. ❧PREHEAT oven to 350°. Cover a damp towel with waxed paper. Unwrap half of the phyllo pastry. Place one sheet of phyllo on waxed paper, brush phyllo sheet with melted butter and sprinkle with finely ground almonds. Place the next sheet on top of the buttered sheet and repeat process. Repeat until all sheets are buttered and sprinkled with ground nuts, and are stacked one on top of another. ❧PLACE half the plum mixture across the bottom third of the stack of phyllo sheets. Fold in left and right sides of phyllo pastry just deep enough to hold in plum mixture before rolling up pastry (about 2 inches on each side). Roll pastry from the bottom up like a jelly roll. Lift towel and waxed paper to start off roll and peel waxed paper gently as you roll up the strudel. ❧PLACE, seam side down, on a buttered baking sheet. Repeat steps 2, 3 and 4 for remaining phyllo sheets and plum filling. Liberally brush strudels with melted butter. With a sharp knife, cut diagonally through top layer of phyllo pastry at two inch intervals. Brush once more with melted butter. Place in oven and bake for 45 minutes. Brush with melted butter every 15 minutes during baking. Remove from oven when strudel is crisp and golden and sprinkle with confectioner's sugar. Serve warm.

Sunday Brunch Puffs

PREPARATION: 10 MIN.   COOKING: 1 HR.   YIELD: 12-16 PUFFS

1 C milk	¼ t pepper
¼ C butter	¼ C Dijon mustard
1 C flour	½ t dry mustard
1 lb. Jarlsberg or Longhorn	2 T caraway seeds
Cheddar cheese, grated	¼ t salt

❧PREHEAT oven to 400°. Line a cookie sheet with waxed paper, grease paper and set aside. ❧MELT butter in a 2-quart saucepan. Add milk and bring to a boil. Lower heat and add flour, salt and pepper all at once. With a wooden spoon, beat mixture over low heat for 1 minute, or until mixture becomes smooth and pulls away from the sides of the pan. ❧REMOVE saucepan from heat and add eggs, *one at a time,* beating after each addition until dough is shiny and smooth. Add cheese, dry mustard and 1 teaspoon of the prepared mustard. ❧DROP batter by heaping tablespoons or pipe through pastry bag into a coffee ring shape onto the prepared, lined, cookie sheet. Bake in oven for 25 minutes or until golden brown. ❧REMOVE from oven. Brush puffs with the remaining Dijon mustard, and sprinkle with caraway seeds. Serve warm.

Sweet Herb Bread

PREPARATION: 2½ HRS.   COOKING: 1 HR.   YIELD: 1 LARGE OR
2 SMALL LOAVES

7 C unbleached white flour
2 pkgs. yeast
⅓ C honey
1 C lukewarm tap water
1 C lukewarm skimmed milk
4 T margarine, melted
  and cooled

1 t dried tarragon
5 eggs
1 T salt
⅔ C fresh parsley, chopped
1 t dried basil
2 bay leaves, crushed

COMBINE warm water and honey in a small bowl. Sprinkle yeast over water and honey mixture and stir gently to dissolve. Meanwhile, combine fresh parsley with salt, basil, tarragon and bay leaves and puree in a food processor or by hand until a paste is formed. Reserve. IN a large bowl, combine the dissolved yeast mixture and the milk and beat until well blended. Add 4 eggs, beating again, until well combined. Begin beating in 4 cups of flour, a cup at a time, then continue beating until dough is very smooth (about 100 strokes). Cover with plastic wrap and let rise in a warm place until doubled in bulk. WHEN dough is doubled in bulk, punch down and fold in the melted margarine and herb paste. Do not beat. Continue folding process, adding the remaining flour as the dough gets sticky. Continue folding process until all ingredients are well combined and dough forms into a ball. PLACE dough on a clean, well floured surface and knead until smooth and elastic. Grease a large bowl. Place kneaded dough in bowl. Cover with plastic wrap and let rise in a warm place until doubled in bulk. PUNCH down dough once again, cover and let rise until doubled in bulk. Punch down, cut dough in half for 2 loaves or leave whole for 1 large loaf. Twist dough into a loose braid and place on greased metal baking sheet. Cover with a towel and leave to rise until doubled in bulk. Preheat oven to 350°. BEAT reserved egg and brush on risen loaves. Bake for 1 hour. Test for doneness by tapping loaves. If they sound hollow, they are done. COOL and serve warm, if possible.

Classic New England Steamed Bread

PREPARATION: 15 MIN.   COOKING: 3 HRS.   YIELD: 2 LOAVES

1 C rye flour
1 C yellow cornmeal
1 C whole wheat flour
1 C whole milk
1 C yogurt

¾ C dark molasses
1½ C raisins
2 t baking soda
Salt to taste
2 (4 C) pudding molds or
   2 (1 lb.) coffee cans, buttered

SIFT rye, cornmeal and whole wheat flours together with salt and baking soda into a mixing bowl. COMBINE milk, yogurt, molasses and raisins and add to flour mixture, beating until thoroughly blended. Spoon dough into buttered molds or coffee cans. Heavily butter heavy-duty foil and cover molds or cans with double layer of foil. Tie a string tightly around foil to secure during steaming process. PLACE rack in a canning pot or other large pot and put sealed molds or cans on rack. Add water to pot so that it comes half-way up the sides of the molds or cans. Cover pot and steam for 3 hours. If water begins to evaporate, add additional hot water. REMOVE cans from water, untie string, remove foil cover and turn bread out onto serving dish. Slice and serve warm.

Hungarian Dessert Crepes

PREPARATION: 15 MIN.   COOKING: 1¼ HRS.   YIELD: 10-12 SERVINGS
(24 CREPES)

5 eggs
1½ C buttermilk (regular or
    light)
2 T butter, melted and cooled
¾ C unbleached flour
¼ t baking soda

¼ t salt
½ C sugar
2 C dried apricots
4 oz. walnuts
⅓ C confectioner's sugar

≈IN a large bowl, combine eggs and buttermilk and whisk to blend thoroughly. Add cooled, melted butter and continue to whisk until mixture is blended. Place flour, baking soda, salt and 2 tablespoons of the sugar in a sifter and sift into the egg mixture. Whisk again to combine all ingredients into a smooth batter. ≈TO prepare crepes, heat a 7½" pan and brush lightly with butter. Turn heat to low-medium setting. Fill a quarter-cup measure halfway with batter and pour onto pan, tilting so that batter spreads to the sides. When edges begin to brown, turn crepe over to brown on reverse side. Do not attempt to turn crepe until it is well set and dry. Turn finished crepes out onto a wax-paper lined surface and stack one on top of another. ≈PLACE apricots in a saucepan with water to cover. Bring to a boil and continue to simmer for half an hour, or until water is absorbed and apricots are tender. Puree apricots, adding remaining sugar. Place 1 heaping tablespoon pureed apricots in each crepe and roll up. Place rolled crepes in a buttered baking dish and heat in oven at 300° for about 15 minutes. ≈MEANWHILE, combine walnuts and confectioner's sugar in blender or food processor and chop nuts coarsely. When crepes are heated through, serve, placing two crepes on each plate and sprinkling each serving with 2 tablespoons of nut mixture.

Old Fashioned Rice Pudding

PREPARATION: 5 MIN.   COOKING: 1½–2 HRS.   YIELD: 6 SERVINGS

1 quart whole milk
½ C sugar
½ C raw long grained rice
1 egg, well beaten

¼ t vanilla
Dash of cinnamon
¼ t nutmeg

COMBINE milk, sugar and rice in a medium saucepan and stir continually over low heat until ingredients thicken. This process will take about an hour and a half and is the secret of rice pudding the way grandmama made it. ADD well beaten egg, vanilla and cinnamon. Stir for another two minutes. SPOON pudding into a large serving bowl or individual dessert cups and sprinkle lightly with nutmeg. Refrigerate until chilled thoroughly.

Gifts
from the
Sea

Section III
&

GIFTS FROM THE SEA

Again, the devil took Him to a very high mountain, and showed Him all the kingdoms of the world and the glory of them; and he said to Him, "All these I will give you, if you will fall down and worship me."

Then Jesus said to him, "Begone, Satan! for it is written, 'You shall worship the Lord your God and Him only shall you serve.'"

Then the devil left Him, and behold, angels came and ministered to Him.

Matthew 4:8–11

In *Much Depends on Dinner* (McClelland and Stewart, Toronto, 1986), the author, Margaret Visser explains that fish is permitted as part of lenten fasting because, unlike meat, eaten by the ancient Greek heroes, fish was considered "mild and non-aggressive within the overall category of flesh ... Lowering one's sights from meat to fish was an exercise in humility, and designed to raise consciousness by elected self-restraint, and by forcing oneself to remember" (pp. 151–152).

Although low on the scale of red and white meats, the fish menus in this section are the most festive of all the foods offered. Here, we celebrate the freedom and communion we have found through our lenten experience of fasting and prayer.

In the third temptation, Jesus is offered dominion over all the kingdoms of the world. To this enticement, he responds by asserting his obedience and service to his Father, and to no other. His trials complete, Jesus is free to be ministered to by angels.

Creamed Salmon on Toast Points

PREPARATION: 5 MIN.　　COOKING: 15 MIN.　　YIELD: 6-8 SERVINGS

1 (16 oz.) can red salmon or　　½ C milk, room temp.
　16 oz. cooked fresh salmon,　　2 T butter
　skinned and deboned　　　　2 T milk
1 pkg. frozen peas　　　　　　¼ t pepper
6-8 slices white bread　　　　Salt to taste

ॐIN a medium saucepan, melt butter over low heat and whisk in the flour until blended. Add the milk and all liquid from salmon can. Increase to moderate heat, and whisk until sauce thickens. If too thick, add a little more milk. ॐREMOVE bones from salmon and stir salmon into sauce. Add peas, correct seasoning, cover and warm thoroughly, stirring to prevent sticking. ॐMEANWHILE, toast bread and cut each slice into fourths. Arrange on individual serving dishes. Spoon creamed salmon over toast points and serve immediately.

Gravlax

PREPARATION: 15 MIN. MARINATING: 2-3 DAYS YIELD: 8-10 SERVINGS

3-3½ lbs. fresh salmon,　　　1 large bunch dill
　thick center cut, boned　　¼ C coarse salt
2 T white peppercorns, crushed　¼ C sugar

ॐSPLIT the center cut of the salmon lengthwise, and remove bones. ॐPLACE half of fish, skin side down, in a deep glass, enamel, or stainless steel dish. Wash and pat dry dill and place on top of fish. Combine sugar, salt and crushed peppercorns and sprinkle evenly over dill. Cover with top half of fish, skin side up. ॐCOVER dish with aluminum foil, place a large, heavy platter over the foil and place 4 cans of food, as weights, on top of platter. ❧REFRIGERATE 2 to 3 days, turning the fish over every 12 hours, and basting each filet of fish with the liquid marinade in the dish. Replace foil, platter and weights after each basting. ❧REMOVE fish from basting dish after 2 or 3 days, when the surface of the flesh looks glazed. Discard dill and gently scrape away seasonings. Pat dry with paper towels. Place each half, skin side down, on a cutting board and thinly slice salmon on the diagonal, carefully separating each slice of fish from skin. ❧SERVE cold or at room temperature with mustard and lemon slices.

Home Smoked Bluefish

Home smoked fish is a rare delicacy that so far outranks the store-bought variety in taste and texture that we have included it here as a way of encouraging more people to try it. Almost any fish will adapt to this recipe. A home smoker can be reasonably purchased through Cabela's, Sidney, Nebraska or L.L.Bean, Freeport, Maine.

PREPARATION: 10 MIN.   COOKING: 14-24 HRS.   YIELD: 15-20
APPETIZERS

1 bluefish, boned, head and tail
   removed (do not remove skin)
2 qts. tap water
1 C coarse Kosher-style salt

½ C light brown sugar
¼ C white vinegar
⅔ t garlic powder
⅔ t onion powder

❧MIX together water, vinegar, sugar and spices. Place bluefish fillet in an enamel or glass roasting pan or casserole. Pour marinade over fish. Let stand 6-12 hours, depending on size of fish. ❧WHEN fish gets a white glaze, remove from marinade, wipe dry with paper towels, and place on smoker. Smoke 8-12 hours with 3 pans of hickory chips. Remove from smoker, wrap in plastic wrap and refrigerate until ready to serve.

Mussels Verde

PREPARATION: 30 MIN.   COOKING: ½ HR.   YIELD: 4 SERVINGS

1 lb. mussels

2 C water

⅓ C dry white wine (or fresh squeezed lemon juice)

⅓ C olive oil

⅓ C chopped onion

⅓ C fresh parsley, chopped

2 T cooked peas

1 t garlic, minced

3 T flour

Salt to taste

꿎PULL whiskers off each mussel and scrub with a vegetable brush to remove sand and hair. Place in a pot of cold water with a teaspoon of cornmeal for 20 minutes. Remove and rinse mussels. Place mussels in a pot with an inch of water at bottom. Bring to a boil, lower flame and simmer until mussels open. Discard any mussels that do not open. 꿎IN a saucepan, heat oil, add onions and saute until transparent. Add flour and mix thoroughly with onions. Add water and wine. Continue cooking, stirring with a whisk until mixture comes to a boil and thickens. Simmer for 3 minutes. 꿎WITH a mortar or electric processor, puree together parsley, peas, garlic and salt, using ¼ cup of simmering wine mixture to thin puree. 꿎WHISK puree mixture into simmering sauce. Stir for 3 minutes. Correct seasoning. 꿎PLACE mussels in a large tureen or individual serving bowls. Spoon sauce over mussels and serve immediately.

Rainbow Trout Salad

This recipe is an excellent way to utilize leftover trout or other fish and can be served as an appetizer or luncheon dish.

PREPARATION: 10 MIN.   YIELD: 4 APPETIZER SERVINGS

2 small rainbow trout, poached or broiled
1 C mayonnaise
¼ C freshly grated or prepared horseradish
2 T ketchup
4 leaves Boston lettuce
4 scallion bulbs, sliced very thin in rounds

COOL trout and carefully fillet and remove skin. Cut each fillet in half horizontally. Combine thoroughly mayonnaise, horseradish and ketchup in small mixing bowl. PLACE a leaf of Boston lettuce on each of four salad plates. Place a fillet of trout on each plate. Spoon 4 or 5 tablespoons of horseradish sauce over each portion of trout and garnish with thinly sliced scallion bulbs. COVER with plastic wrap and refrigerate until ready to serve.

Squid Salad Trattoria

PREPARATION: 10 MIN.   COOKING: 15 MIN.   YIELD: 4-6 SERVINGS

1 lb. fresh squid, cleaned and
   cut into strips
6 T olive oil
1 clove garlic, minced
¼ C vinegar

Salt and pepper to taste
½ Spanish onion, diced fine
½ lemon, cut in thin wedges
2 t finely chopped parsley
   to garnish

IN a medium skillet, heat oil, add garlic and saute one minute. Add strips of squid and tentacles, cut up, and stir to coat in oil. Lower flame and continue sauteing until tender, about 15 minutes. WITH a slotted spoon, remove squid from skillet and place in a mixing bowl. Add vinegar, onion and salt and pepper. REFRIGERATE, covered until chilled. Serve in a shell or shrimp icer with lemon wedge and chopped parsley to garnish.

Tangy Salmon Mousse

PREPARATION: 20 MIN. CHILLING TIME: 5 HRS. YIELD: 6-8 SERVINGS

2 C fresh salmon, poached, flaked,
   deboned and skinned, or canned
1 envelope gelatine
¼ C cold water
½ C boiling water
½ C mayonnaise

1 T fresh lemon juice
1 t grated onion
½ t tabasco sauce
¼ t paprika
Salt to taste
1½ C ricotta cheese

IN a mixing bowl, soften gelatin in cold water, add boiling water, and stir until dissolved. Cool to room temperature. Add mayonnaise, lemon juice, onion, tabasco, paprika and salt. Refrigerate until chilled and thickened to the consistency of beaten egg yolks. Remove from refrigerator and fold in flaked salmon. Combine thoroughly. IN a blender whip ricotta cheese until smooth and creamy. Add salmon mixture and blend until smooth. With a rubber spatula fold mousse into a greased 1½ quart mold. (A fish mold is particularly attractive for this dish.) CHILL in refrigerator for 5 hours until set. Unmold and serve with sesame crackers or pumpernickel rounds.

Basic Fish Stock

Whenever buying or catching fish, save heads, tails, bones and skin. These may be used immediately to make a hearty fish stock or wrapped in plastic bags and frozen for later use. Also, ask your fish market for the scraps they usually throw away.

PREPARATION: 10 MIN.   COOKING: ½ HR.   YIELD: 2 CUPS

4-6 C fish trimmings (heads, bones and/or skin)
1 medium onion, sliced thin
¼ C carrots, sliced thin
½ bay leaf
6-8 parsley sprigs with stems
¼ t salt
Water

❧PLACE all ingredients in a saucepan and add enough water to cover. Simmer, uncovered for 30 minutes or until liquid reduces to about 2 cups. ❧STRAIN stock through a fine-meshed sieve. Correct seasonings to taste. ❧USE immediately, refrigerate for a day or freeze for several weeks.

Bouillabaisse St. Tropez

PREPARATION: 15 MIN.   COOKING: 35 MIN.   YIELD: 6 SERVINGS

2½ quarts fish stock
1 C clam juice
1 small lobster, cut up
6 mussels, cleaned & scrubbed
12 medium shrimp
6 clams, cleaned & scrubbed
2 crabs, cleaned and cut up
1 lb. deboned white-flesh fish
  (cod, halibut, haddock, etc.)
1 small leek, sliced in rounds
½ C olive oil
4 cloves garlic, minced and mashed

1 small can tomatoes, diced
2 T tomato paste
1 bay leaf
¼ t leaf thyme
¼ t fennel
1 T chopped parsley
¼ t saffron
¼ t minced orange peel
2 T flour
2 T butter
Salt and pepper to taste

🍂IN a large stock pot, make a roux with 2 tablespoons melted butter and 2 tablespoons of flour. Add stock and clam juice. Bring to a boil. Add seasoning and, except for fish, all remaining ingredients. Cover and bring to a boil. Lower heat and simmer for 10 minutes. 🍂ADD white fish and simmer rapidly for 5 minutes. Add all shellfish and cook until done, 7 to 8 minutes. 🍂REMOVE fish from pot and place in a large soup tureen. Correct seasoning in stock and pour stock over fish in tureen. 🍂GARNISH with sprigs of parsley and serve. Pass Parmesan cheese and crusty French bread.

Down East Clam Chowder

PREPARATION: 20 MIN.   COOKING: 45 MIN.   YIELD: 10 CUPS OR
4 MAIN SERVINGS

2 T vegetable oil
2 medium onions, sliced thin
3 doz. cherrystone clams, shucked,
   with liquid reserved
2 T flour
3 large potatoes, peeled and
   diced

¼ t celery salt
¼ t pepper
3 C milk
2 T butter
¼ C finely chopped
   parsley or chives
Salt to taste

❧IN a large saucepan or Dutch oven, over medium heat, saute onions in oil until tender, about 5 minutes. Do not brown onions. ❧CHOP clams and reserve. Add enough water to clam liquid to make 2 cups. Stir flour into onion mixture until blended. Gradually stir in clam liquid mixture and cook, stirring constantly, until mixture is slightly thickened. Stir in potatoes, celery salt and pepper. ❧COVER and cook until potatoes are tender, about 10 minutes. Add clams, milk and butter; cover and cook until heated through, about 10 minutes, stirring often. ❧SERVE piping hot, and garnish to taste with finely chopped parsley or chives.

Hampton Bays Fish Chowder

PREPARATION: 20 MIN.   COOKING: 30 MIN.   YIELD: 6 SERVINGS

2 lbs. "catch of the day" fish or
   2 dozen clams, minced
4 T vegetable oil
2 medium onions, chopped
6 medium potatoes, peeled
   and diced
½ green pepper, chopped

½ C celery, chopped
4 C tomatoes, chopped or
   2 C tomato juice
Salt to taste
⅛ t cayenne
⅛ t sage
⅛ t thyme leaf

≈HEAT oil in a large saucepan or Dutch oven. Add onion, celery and green peppers and saute lightly for about 5 minutes, stirring to keep vegetables from browning. Add tomatoes, potatoes and fish. Add water to cover. ≈COVER saucepan and bring to a boil. Lower heat, add spices, return, cover and simmer for about 10 minutes, or until fish flakes. Remove fish with a slotted spoon and continue simmering soup until potatoes are tender, about 10 minutes more. ≈MEANWHILE, remove and discard bones and skin of fish. Cut fish into bite size pieces and return to soup pot. If using minced clams, add them to the pot now. ≈SIMMER another 5 minutes and serve piping hot.

Louisiana Okra Gumbo

PREPARATION: 15 MIN.   COOKING: 3 HRS.   YIELD: 8-10 SERVINGS

1½ lbs. small okra pods
2 large onions chopped
½ green pepper, chopped
2 cloves garlic, minced
2-4 T vegetable oil
1 T flour
2 t cider vinegar
1½ qts. fish stock
Salt and pepper to taste

1½ lbs. white-flesh fish
   (cod, haddock, etc.) cut
   into 1" cubes
6 small hard-shelled crabs
2 lbs. small shrimp
1 (4 oz.) can tomato sauce
2 bay leaves
8 C steamed white rice

≈WASH and dry okra and discard the topmost part of stem, taking care not to cut into pod. Combine with onions, green peppers and garlic in a mixing bowl and set aside. ≈IN a large Dutch oven, heat oil. Sprinkle flour over oil and stir to make a light roux, the consistency of milk. Add okra and vegetable mixture and simmer, uncovered, for 20 minutes over moderate heat. Stir and turn frequently to prevent okra from scorching. ≈AFTER 20 minutes, add vinegar and stir. If the mixture is dry, add a little more oil. Keep heat moderate and continue simmering for 10 more minutes. Stir frequently. Okra mixture, when ready, will have the consistency of thick oatmeal. ❧ADD tomato sauce and 2 cups of hot tap water. Add fish stock, bay leaves, salt and pepper. Cover and bring to a lively boil and then reduce heat. If soup is becoming too thick, boil water and add to pot as needed. Simmer slowly for 2 hours. Add cubed fish and crabs and continue to simmer for 15 minutes. Add shrimp and continue simmering until fish is no longer translucent. ❧SERVE hot in soup plates over a scant cup of rice.

❧

VEGETABLES AND SALADS

Braised Potatoes

PREPARATION: 15 MIN.   COOKING: 45 MIN.   YIELD: 5 SERVINGS

5 medium potatoes	1½ C plum tomatoes,
4 T vegetable oil	chopped
1 medium onion, chopped	3 T fresh parsley, chopped
2 cloves garlic, minced	Salt and pepper to taste

❧PEEL, quarter and soak potatoes in cold water. ❧HEAT oil in medium frying pan and saute onions until soft. Add garlic; drain and add potatoes, and stir for a minute on medium heat. Add tomatoes and enough water to cover potatoes, if needed. Stir in parsley and add salt and pepper. ❧SIMMER, covered, over low heat for 30 minutes. Uncover and continue cooking over low heat, turning occasionally, until potatoes are tender and sauce thickened. ❧SERVE warm.

Cantonese Fried Rice

PREPARATION: 10 MIN.   COOKING: 35 MIN.   YIELD: 4-6 SERVINGS

2 C cold, cooked white rice
1 large onion, chopped
2⅓ T vegetable oil
½ bunch of scallions, sliced in
    rounds (with green tops)

2 eggs, well beaten
2 C bean sprouts, washed
    and drained
¼ C soy sauce
¼ t white pepper
Salt and pepper to taste

❧HEAT a teaspoon of oil in a small skillet. Add beaten eggs and scramble lightly. Remove eggs from heat, and with a fork, break eggs into small pieces. Set aside. ❧IN a deep skillet, heat 2 tablespoons of oil and add onion. Saute until golden. Add rice and stir until grains are well coated with oil and turn slightly tan in color. Add pepper and soy sauce. ❧CORRECT seasoning and add salt if needed and extra soy sauce to taste. Add bean sprouts, scallions and reserved scrambled eggs. Stir to combine thoroughly. Cover again and continue to cook until done. Serve piping hot.

Carrots and Turnips Canadienne

PREPARATION: 20 MIN.   COOKING: 20 MIN.   YIELD: 6-8 SERVINGS

1 lb. carrots, cut into ¾″ cubes
1 medium yellow turnip, cut into ¾″ cubes
¼ lb. butter or margarine
4 sprigs of parsley, chopped fine
Salt and pepper to taste

❧IN a 3-4 quart saucepan, combine cubed carrots and turnips and add water to cover. Bring water to a boil and lower heat. Cover saucepan and simmer vegetables for about 20 minutes, or until carrots and turnips can be pierced with a fork but are still crunchy.

PLACE vegetables into a shallow serving bowl, add butter and salt and pepper to taste. Toss to coat vegetables with butter. GARNISH dish with chopped parsley and serve immediately.

Mediterranean Fried Vegetables

This garlic sauce is good with any fried foods.

PREPARATION: 30 MIN.   COOKING: 30 MIN.   YIELD: 6 SERVINGS

2 medium zucchini, scrubbed
and sliced in ¼" rounds
2 small eggplants, scrubbed
and sliced in ¼" rounds
1 C flour
2 C vegetable oil

Garlic Sauce
6-7 cloves garlic
4 medium potatoes, peeled,
boiled and mashed
1 C olive oil
⅓ C white vinegar
Salt and pepper to taste

CRUSH garlic with a dash of salt in an electric processor or hand mortar. Add mashed potatoes to mixmaster bowl or the processor container and blend well with garlic. Alternately add oil and vinegar, beating until well blended. Reserve. If you desire a thinner sauce, add up to 1 cup of fish or vegetable stock. HEAT oil in medium sized skillet. Dredge prepared vegetable rounds in flour and brown in well-heated oil. Turn and brown on other side. REMOVE vegetables with a slotted spatula and drain on paper towels. SERVE hot or at room temperature and pass garlic sauce as garnish.

Calico Health Salad

3 lbs. cabbage, shredded coarsely
2 medium green peppers, cut in rings
2 medium red peppers, cut in rings
2 large red Spanish onions, cut in rings
½ C sugar

1 t dry mustard
1 t celery seeds
1 C white vinegar
⅔ C safflower oil
Salt and pepper to taste

COMBINE ¼ cup of sugar, mustard, celery seeds, salt, pepper, vinegar and oil in a saucepan. Bring to a rolling boil, stirring continually. Remove from heat. TOSS cabbage, peppers and onions in a large bowl with the remaining ¼ cup of sugar, and add heated vinegar dressing. Cover bowl and refrigerate overnight. BEFORE serving, toss with salad forks to combine salad with any dressing that has settled on the bottom.

Classic Greek Salad

1 head lettuce, chicory, escarole
    or other greens
1 cucumber, cubed
2 tomatoes, cubed
1 green pepper, cubed
6 radishes, sliced
3 scallions or 1 small Spanish
    onion, sliced

10 black olives
5-10 anchovy fillets
½ C feta cheese, crumbled
¾ C olive oil
¼ C wine vinegar
1-2 T dry oregano leaves
Garlic powder to taste
Salt and pepper to taste

IN a serving bowl, gently toss together first nine ingredients. IN a small mixing bowl, whisk together oil, vinegar, oregano, salt and pepper until thoroughly combined. TOSS salad with dressing until combined and serve immediately.

Wild Garden Salad

PREPARATION: 10 MIN.   COOKING: 15-20 MIN.   YIELD: 4-6 SERVINGS

1 bunch dandelion, chicory or arugula greens
2 T oil
Juice of half a lemon
1 clove garlic chopped
2 anchovies, chopped fine (optional)
Salt and pepper to taste

&IF using dandelion greens, steam in microwave in a covered dish just until tender. Drain thoroughly, cool and slice in strips. Place in salad bowl. If using arugula, chicory or escarole, wash thoroughly and tear into bite-sized pieces. Place in salad bowl. &COMBINE remaining ingredients in a small mixing bowl. Pour dressing over prepared greens and toss to combine. Serve immediately.

&

MAIN DISHES

Baked Butterfly of Bass

PREPARATION: 30 MIN.   COOKING: 50-60 MIN.   YIELD: 4-6 SERVINGS

1 (5 lb.) farm raised striped bass, boned
1 lb. medium shrimp, shelled, de-veined and diced
1 carrot, sliced
½ C celery, minced
¼ C shallots, minced
Salt and pepper to taste
½ C fresh parsley, chopped fine
1¾ C dry white wine
1½ C diced day-old white bread
1 bay leaf
1½ sticks of butter

IN a medium skillet, melt 1 stick of butter and add 2 tablespoons minced shallots and half-cup of minced celery. Saute until shallots are soft. Add shrimp and parsley and saute over gentle heat until shrimp turn pink. Remove skillet from heat. Combine diced bread and 2 tablespoons of white wine with shrimp mixture and mix until bread is evenly moist. Add salt and pepper to taste. PREHEAT oven to 375°. Rinse fish and pat dry with paper towels. Rub inner flesh of fish with salt and pepper and stuff with reserved shrimp mixture. Seal opening with skewers and double thickness of thread. PLACE sliced carrot and celery, remaining minced shallots and bay leaf on the bottom of a large casserole dish. Place fish over vegetables and add remaining wine. Melt remaining half-stick of butter and brush on fish. Place casserole in preheated 375° oven and bake, uncovered, for about an hour or until fish flakes easily, basting fish every fifteen minutes with pan juices. Remove from casserole to serving dish. Pour pan juices and vegetables into a gravy boat and serve as a garnish with fish.

Baked Shrimp à la Greque

PREPARATION: 25 MIN.   COOKING: 30 MIN.   YIELD: 4 SERVINGS

3 T vegetable oil
2 C chopped Bermuda onions
1 clove garlic, minced
¼ C fresh parsley, chopped fine
2 T fresh dill, chopped fine
1½ C feta cheese, crumbled

¼ t dry mustard
5 T tomato paste diluted in
    ¾ C hot water
1 lb. medium shrimp, peeled
    and de-veined

PREHEAT oven to 450°. In small saucepan, heat oil and saute onions until wilted. Add garlic, parsley, dill, mustard and diluted tomato paste. Cover and simmer for 15 minutes. ADD shrimp and stir until shrimp are well-coated with sauce, about 1 minute. SPOON shrimp mixture into a 1½ quart casserole dish and sprinkle with crumbled feta cheese. PLACE in 450° oven and bake for 15 minutes or until cheese softens.

Grilled Trout Provençale

PREPARATION: 10 MIN. COOKING: 20-30 MIN. YIELD: 4-6 SERVINGS

4 fillets of salmon, trout or sea trout
2 T vegetable oil
2 cloves garlic, minced
2 sprigs fresh parsley, chopped very fine
¼ C olive oil
Juice of half a lemon
Salt and pepper to taste

❧HEAT grill or broiler to high heat. Place fish on grill or in a pan under broiler. Brush with vegetable oil and sprinkle with salt and pepper. Grill for 20 to 30 minutes without turning. ❧WHILE fish is grilling, beat together olive oil, lemon juice and garlic until thickened. This can be done with a whisk or electric blender. Add chopped parsley and pour sauce into a serving dish. ❧REMOVE fish from grill or broiler when it is brown and crisp and easy to flake with a fork. Place on serving platter and pass the sauce.

Salt Cod Stew

PREPARATION: 20 MIN.   COOKING: 1 HR.   YIELD: 4-6 SERVINGS

1½ lbs. dry salt cod
1 C olive oil
½ C chopped parsley
1 C tomatoes, fresh or canned, chopped
1 lb. onions, chopped
1 clove garlic, minced
½ C hot water
Salt and pepper to taste

❧CUT dry salt cod in 2-inch squares. Wash thoroughly in cold water, place in a large bowl, cover with cold water and soak overnight. ❧NEXT day, heat ½ cup of olive oil in a saucepan. Add garlic and saute for 1 minute. Add onions and saute until golden. Add tomatoes, parsley, seasoning and water. Cover saucepan and simmer for 10 minutes. ❧SPREAD stewed tomatoes and onions in the bottom of a 2-quart baking dish. Rinse codfish in cold water, pat dry and arrange on top of stewed tomatoes and onions. Bake in a 350° oven for 45 minutes. Check moisture level and add a little water if needed. ❧SERVE piping hot with tiny boiled potatoes and buttered peas.

Seafood Pastry Supreme

PREPARATION: 1 HR.   COOKING: 2½ HRS.   YIELD: 6-8 SERVINGS

2½ lbs. cod (boned, skinned and cubed)	1 onion, minced
	5 cloves garlic, minced
1 lb. tiny frozen uncooked shrimp	½ t basil
1 lb. mozzarella cheese, grated (regular or light)	½ t oregano
	1 t salt
1 lb. phyllo pastry leaves	¼ t pepper
1 lb. sweet butter, melted	4 T olive oil
2 C bread crumbs	2 T butter, melted
¼ C grated Romano cheese	2 T flour
¼ C grated Parmesan cheese	½ C dry white wine
¼ C fresh parsley, chopped very fine	1½ C boiling water or hot fish stock
4 C fresh tomatoes, chopped fine	3 T tomato paste

❧IN a medium saucepan, heat 2 tablespoons of oil, and 1½ teaspoons minced garlic (about 2 cloves) and saute 1 minute. Add onion, and saute until onion browns. Stir to keep onion from scorching and scrape bottom of saucepan to release caramelized onion drippings, which add flavor to the sauce. Add chopped tomatoes, tomato paste, basil, oregano, salt and pepper. Bring to a boil, cover saucepan, lower heat, and simmer slowly for about 1 hour. Stir occasionally. When tomatoes have cooked down to a thick sauce, remove saucepan from heat and set aside. ❧IN a deep skillet, heat the remaining 2 tablespoons of olive oil. Saute remaining minced garlic for 1 minute. Add cubes of cod and stir gently until fish is coated with oil. Add dry white wine and boiling water or stock. Cover skillet and poach cod on low flame for 10 minutes or until fish is just tender. Add frozen shrimp; Cover skillet and poach another 5 minutes, or until shrimp turn pink. Remove cod and shrimp to a bowl with a slotted spoon. Reserve all poaching liquid from skillet in a small saucepan. ❧IN a medium-sized mixing bowl, combine bread crumbs, grated Romano and Parmesan cheeses and finely chopped parsley. Cover a damp kitchen towel with waxed paper. Remove half of the pastry leaves from the package. Place one sheet of phyllo on waxed paper. With a pastry brush, brush phyllo sheet with melted butter and sprinkle with bread crumb mixture. Place the next sheet of pastry on top of the buttered sheet and repeat process. Repeat until all sheets are buttered and sprinkled with bread crumb mixture and are stacked one on top of another. ❧PLACE half of the seafood across the bottom third of the stack of phyllo sheets. Spoon half of the reserved tomato sauce over the fish and sprinkle with half of the grated mozzarella cheese. Fold in left and right sides of phyllo pastry just deep enough to hold in the seafood mixture before rolling up pastry (about 2 inches on each side). Roll pastry from the bottom up, like a jelly roll. Lift towel and waxed paper to start off roll and peel waxed paper gently as you roll up the pastry. ❧PLACE, seam side down, on a buttered baking sheet. Liberally brush pastry roll with melted butter and sprinkle with 2 tablespoons of bread crumb mixture. With a sharp knife, cut diagonally through top layer of phyllo pastry at 2-inch intervals. Brush once more with melted butter. ❧PREHEAT oven to 350°. Proceed as described in preceding paragraphs for remaining sheets of phyllo, using up remaining seafood, tomato sauce, grated mozzarella cheese and bread crumb mixture. Place both pastry rolls in oven and bake for 45 minutes. Brush with melted butter every 15 minutes during baking. Remove from oven when pastry is crisp and golden. Serve at once. ❧WHILE seafood pastry is baking, make a roux by whisking 2 tablespoons of melted butter with 2 tablespoons of flour. Combine dry white wine in saucepan with reserved poaching liquid and add salt and pepper to taste. Over low heat, whisk in roux until sauce thickens slightly. Place in gravy boat, and serve with seafood pastry.

Skewered Seafood

PREPARATION: 20 MIN.　COOKING: 15 MIN.　YIELD: 4–6 SERVINGS

3 lbs. deboned fish (bluefish,
　tile fish, swordfish, shark
　or fresh tuna), cut in
　1 inch cubes
12 tiny white onions
12 cherry tomatoes
12 button mushrooms

2 green peppers, cut into
　1-inch cubes
6 T　white vinegar
6 T　olive oil
1 t　salt
¼ t　pepper
1 t　oregano

THREAD skewers alternately with fish and vegetables. COMBINE vinegar, oil and seasoning in a shallow dish. Place skewered seafood and vegetables in marinade. Refrigerate for 2 hours, turning and basting skewers every half-hour. COOK for 15 minutes on a hot outdoor grill or broil in the oven at high heat. Baste with marinade while cooking. Serve with a rice pilaf.

Spanish Scallops

PREPARATION: 15 MIN.　COOKING: 45 MIN.　YIELD: 4 SERVINGS

1 quart bay scallops
¼ C　olive oil
1 large Spanish onion, sliced fine
1½ C　long grain white rice
Salt and pepper to taste

3 C　boiling water
Pinch of saffron
½ C　chopped fresh parsley
　for garnish

WASH scallops. In a medium skillet, heat oil and saute onions until wilted and golden. ADD scallops and saute for 2 minutes. Cover skillet and cook over moderate heat for 15 minutes. Stir occasionally to prevent scorching. ✒ADD rice to skillet and stir grains until lightly tanned. Add 3 cups boiling water and spices and bring to a boil. Lower heat, cover skillet and simmer for 15 minutes. ✒REMOVE skillet from heat and leave to stand, covered, for 5 minutes. Serve at once with chopped parsley as a garnish.

Steamed Fish with Ginger Sauce

PREPARATION: 15 MIN.　　COOKING: 20 MIN.　　YIELD: 4 SERVINGS

1 sea bass or red snapper (about 3 lbs.)
1 T dry cooking sherry
2 scallions, washed, split lengthwise
  and cut into 1½" long pieces
2 T finely shredded ginger root
3 T vegetable oil
3 T light soy sauce
½ t sugar

✒CLEAN and wash fish and pat dry with paper towels. Slash the fish on both sides across the belly with a sharp knife. Place whole fish in a dish and sprinkle with sherry. Let stand 5 minutes. ✒MEANWHILE, cover bottom of steamer with 1½ inches of water and bring to a boil. Place fish on steaming rack. Cover tightly and steam over high heat for 12-15 minutes. ✒IN a skillet or wok, heat vegetable oil on high heat. Add shredded ginger and lower heat to medium. Fry ginger for 1 minute. Add scallions and stir fry for 12 seconds. Add soy sauce and sugar. Stir once and remove from heat. ✒REMOVE fish from steamer and place on platter. Pour ginger sauce over fish and serve piping hot.

Almond Lace

PREPARATION: 10 MIN.   COOKING: 1 HR.   YIELD: 1 DOZEN

½ C flour
⅓ C light corn syrup
½ C confectioner's sugar
¼ lb. sweet butter, sliced thin
1 T finely chopped blanched almonds
2 drops almond extract

❧IN a small saucepan, over low heat, combine corn syrup, sugar and butter slices and stir until butter melts. Remove saucepan from heat and with a whisk, beat in the flour until thoroughly combined. Add chopped almonds and extract and continue to whisk until mixture is fully blended. Set mixture aside for 10 minutes. ❧MEANWHILE, preheat oven to 350° and thickly butter two cookie sheets. ❧FOR each almond lace, place 2 level tablespoons of almond mixture on a cookie sheet and place in oven. Bake until golden about 8 minutes. You may place two cookie sheets in one oven. Remove from oven, cool for a few minutes and, using a flat metal spatula and your hands, remove lace cookie from sheet and shape as desired. Continue process until mixture is used up. When shaping lace cookies into funnels or into creative free-form designs, timing is the key to success. If the cookie is too hot, it will collapse into a sticky glob when removed from the baking sheet. If the cookie has cooled too much, it will be brittle and crumble when being shaped. To avoid either problem, allow cookie to cool for about 2 minutes before attempting to shape. If cookie does collapse or become too brittle, return to oven for a minute or two and it will become workable again. ❧PRESENT lace in a doily-lined, shallow basket or in a decorative, shallow serving bowl.

Baklava

PREPARATION: 1 HR.   COOKING: 1–1½ HRS.   YIELD: 3 DOZEN

1 lb. phyllo pastry sheets
1 lb. sweet butter, melted
½ lb. walnuts, chopped
½ lb. blanched almonds, ground
3 C sugar

1 C water
Juice of half a lemon, strained
¼ peel of an orange
2 dashes of ground cloves
Baking pan 15″ × 10″ × 1¼″

❧IN a buttered baking pan 15″ × 10″ × 1¼″, place a sheet of phyllo and brush with melted butter. Repeat for another 11 sheets of pastry. Combine chopped almonds and walnuts in a small bowl, and spread ⅓ of this mixture over the phyllo. ❧PREHEAT oven to 325°. Place another sheet of phyllo over the nut mixture and brush with melted butter. Repeat for another 3 sheets of pastry. Sprinkle another ⅓ of the nut mixture over the phyllo. Repeat process with 4 more sheets of phyllo, ending up with the remaining nut mixture. Cover the nut mixture with remaining sheets of phyllo, brushing each sheet with butter after placing it in the pan. ❧WITH a very sharp knife, cut through the phyllo to shape into 3 dozen diamond shaped pieces. Place in oven and bake until golden brown, up to 1½ hours. Remove from oven. ❧MEANWHILE, in a saucepan, combine sugar, water, lemon juice, orange peel and ground cloves and bring to a boil. Boil for 10 minutes, remove from heat and cool. When syrup is cold, pour over steaming hot baklava. Cool overnight before serving.

Heavenly Lemony Angel Food Cake

PREPARATION: 30 MIN.   COOKING: 50 MIN.   YIELD: 8-10 SERVINGS

1¾ C egg whites (about 14), at room temperature
1¼ C flour (sifted before measuring)
1¾ C granulated sugar
½ t salt
1½ t cream of tartar
1 t vanilla extract

¼ t almond extract
2 T butter
2 T milk
2½ C confectioner's sugar
3 T lemon juice, freshly squeezed
Grated rind of 1 lemon

❧PREHEAT oven to 375°. Sift flour with ¾ cup of the granulated sugar. Resift 3 more times. ❧IN a large bowl, beat egg whites with salt and cream of tartar until soft peaks form. Slowly add the remaining cup of granulated sugar while continuing to beat, adding ¼ cup at a time. Beat egg whites until very stiff peaks form. With a rubber spatula, gently fold vanilla and almond extracts into egg whites. ❧SIFT flour mixture, ¼ cup at a time over egg whites. Fold each addition of flour gently into egg whites with a rubber spatula. To make sure your angel cake batter does not collapse, be very careful not to overwork the batter when folding the flour into the egg whites. The success of the cake rests primarily on this step. Using the rubber spatula, gently scoop batter into an ungreased 10-inch tube pan. Cut through the batter twice with a knife. Smooth top of batter with a rubber spatula and spread batter so that it touches the sides of the pan. ❧BAKE in preheated oven on lower rack for 35 to 40 minutes or until cake springs back when pressed gently with finger tip. Remove cake from oven and invert pan over the neck of a bottle. Cool completely, about 2 hours. Loosen from pan with a rubber spatula and place on cake plate. ❧IN a medium saucepan over very low heat, warm butter and milk until butter melts. Do not let it come to a boil. Remove from heat. Stir in confectioner's sugar and stir until sugar is totally dissolved and very smooth. Beat in lemon juice and grated rind. Set aside to cool until just thick enough to spread. Spread immediately, once thickened, over top and sides of angel food cake.

Kourambiethes
(Greek Wedding Cookies)

PREPARATION: 30 MIN.   COOKING: 10-15 MIN.   YIELD: 3 DOZEN

1 lb. sweet butter
1½ C confectioner's sugar
4½ C flour
1 egg yolk

2 T cognac
1 t vanilla
1 t baking powder
Whole cloves

❧PREHEAT oven to 325°. With an electric mixer at high speed, beat butter and 6 tablespoons of confectioner's sugar together for 20 minutes or until almost white in color. ❧BY hand, add 4½ cups of flour until dough forms a soft ball. Shape dough into walnut-sized balls, place clove in center of each ball, and place on buttered baking sheets. Bake in preheated oven for 10 to 15 minutes or until light brown. ❧SPRINKLE powdered sugar on waxed paper. Remove from oven and cool on waxed paper. When slightly cooled, sift confectioner's sugar over cookies to coat. ❧THESE crumbly, delicate cookies improve with age and should be made at least a week in advance. In an airtight container, they will stay good for 4 to 6 weeks. Kourambiethes freeze exceptionally well. Place them between layers of waxed paper in a plastic container. When ready to use, remove them from the freezer, leave them at room temperature for an hour and serve.

Zeppole di San Giuseppe

PREPARATION: 15 MIN.   COOKING: 1 HR.   YIELD: 18 PUFFS

1 C water
½ C butter
1 T sugar
½ t salt
4 eggs

1 C all-purpose flour, sifted
1 t grated orange rind
1 t grated lemon rind
2 C whipped cream
¼ t vanilla

❧COMBINE water, butter, sugar and salt in a saucepan. Bring to a boil, remove pan from heat, and add flour all at once. With wooden spoon, stir flour mixture until it leaves the sides of the pan and forms a ball around the spoon. ❧ADD 1 egg, beat vigorously, until mixture is glossy and smooth. Repeat, 1 egg at a time, until all 4 eggs are added. ❧ADD grated rinds, and combine thoroughly. ❧DROP mixture by rounded tablespoonfuls, 2 inches apart, onto greased baking sheet. Bake at 450° for 15 minutes. Lower oven temperature to 350° and bake 25 minutes longer. ❧COOL completely and cut slit in side of each puff. Combine whipped cream and vanilla and fill pastries.

Creole Bread Pudding

PREPARATION: 15 MIN.   COOKING: 1½ HR.   YIELD: 8 SERVINGS

1 French bread, cut into
   1½"-2" slices
1 lb. sweet butter, at room temp.
2 C sugar
5 eggs
13 ounces evaporated milk
2¼ C skim milk
3 t nutmeg

1 T cinnamon
⅔ C raisins
1 T grated lemon peel
Juice of ½ lemon
3 T canned shredded
   coconut
2 T vanilla

❧IN a mixing bowl, with electric mixer on high speed, cream ½ pound butter and ⅔ cup of sugar until very fluffy. Add 3 eggs, one at a time, beating after each addition. Slowly beat in all the milk and the evaporated milk until fully blended. Add vanilla and nutmeg to milk mixture and stir to combine. Fold in raisins, coconut and lemon peel. Pour this mixture into 9 × 13-inch pan. ❧PREHEAT oven to 350°. Place prepared slices of French bread in egg and milk mixture and let stand for 15 minutes, or until bread has absorbed most of the liquid. Very gently fold pudding with a wooden spoon in over and under movements to fully combine softened bread, raisins and custard mixture. Press down on bread with spoon to make sure remaining liquid covers bread in casserole. Sprinkle with cinnamon. ❧PLACE in oven until custard sets and top is golden brown, up to 1½ hours. Remove from oven and cool to room temperature. ❧MEANWHILE, in a double boiler over hot water, melt remaining ½ pound of butter. In a small bowl, beat together remaining 1⅓ cups of sugar and remaining 2 eggs until thickened. Whisk egg mixture into melted butter in double boiler. Continue whisking for 3 minutes until sugar melts and sauce is thickened. Remove saucepan from hot water. Whisk for 4 minutes, or until slightly cool. Stir in juice of ½ lemon and nutmeg. ❧TO serve, spoon pudding into individual serving plates and liberally pour sauce over pudding.

Index